HARLEY-DAVIDSON
POLICE MOTORCYCLES

Robert and Robin Genat

Dedication

To Hans, a generous friend and mentor

First published in 1995 by Motorbooks International Publishers & Wholesalers, 729 Prospect Avenue, PO box 1, Osceola, WI 54020-0001 USA

© Robert Genat and Robin Genat, 1995

All rights reserved. With the exception of quoting brief passages for the purposes of review no part of this publication may be reproduced without prior written permission from the Publisher

Motorbooks International is a certified trademark, registered with the United States Patent Office

The information in this book is true and complete to the best of our knowledge. All recommendations are made without any guarantee on the part of the author or Publisher, who also disclaim any liability incurred in connection with the use of this data or specific details

We recognize that some words, model names and designations, for example, mentioned herein are the property of the trademark holder. We use them for identification purposes only. This is not an official publication

Motorbooks International books are also available at discounts in bulk quantity for industrial or sales-promotional use. For details write to Special Sales Manager at the Publisher's address

Library of Congress Cataloging-in-Publication Data

Genat, Robert
    Harley-Davidson police motorcycles /
    Robert Genat and Robin Genat.
        p. cm.
    Includes index.
    ISBN 0-7603-0066-6 (pbk.)
    1. Harley-Davidson motorcycle--History.
    2. Police vehicles--History. I. Title.
TL448.H3G45   1995
629.227'5--dc20   95-14002

On the front cover: This motor officer hails from Wichita Falls, Kansas. *Harley-Davidson Archives*

On the back cover: **Top:** Two Milwaukee officers with brand-new 1962 Harley-Davidson motorcycles, a Duo-Glide and a Servi-Car. *Harley-Davidson Archives*

Below: Californian Highway Patrol training took some bizarre turns, as evidenced by this photo of an officer firing from behind his overturned motorcycle. *Harley-Davidson Archives*

Printed and bound in the United States of America

CONTENTS

ACKNOWLEDGMENTS

Our research began in a small, temporary storage area in the basement of Harley-Davidson Motor Company's beautiful corporate offices on Juneau Avenue in Milwaukee. Archivist Dr. Martin Jack Rosenblum was in the early stages of establishing a formal historical services department and a museum. Under his watchful eye, we reverently fingered volumes of photographs of police motorcycles. Permeated by the Harley myth, we felt as though we had entered some ancient cave whose wall paintings held untold stories and secrets. Our thanks and appreciation to all who hosted us during our short visit.

We are also indebted to the many police and motor officers nationwide who managed to locate archival photographs and dusty journals to share with us. Many officers were astounded to realize that their departments had little or no historical information on hand. When the officers did locate photographs, the images often lacked complete captions or background information. In those cases, we did the best we could to establish dates and models. Many departments, however, had volumes of photos, a designated department historian, or maintained a department museum. For the most part, these folks did a lot of digging! If we mention a particular department by name, we do so as a way of illustrating what may have been going on in other agencies throughout the country during that same time frame.

About one-third of the photographs in this book were reproduced from priceless originals using digital technology, including a Macintosh Quadra 650, a Color OneScanner, and Adobe Photoshop. Because of this technology, we were able to scan archival photos into our computer, creating a digital copy on a computer disk. We could manipulate the digital image, including cropping, enlarging, repairing, and enhancing, in ways that are usually not possible without an original negative. Scanning the photos also enabled us to convince police officers and collectors to part with their originals for a few days, sending them certified mail in both directions for safety. The publisher printed these photos from the computer disk. Hats off to Motorbooks for allowing us to submit a large portion of these photos on computer disk!

We acknowledge the following good people who went out of their way to participate in this project:

Harley-Davidson Motor Company, Incorporated:

Jon Syverson, International Fleet Sales Manager

Dr. Martin Jack Rosenblum, Archivist and Museum Curator

Law Enforcement Agencies Nationwide:

Sgt. Dave Zuhlke, Springfield (Missouri) Police Dept.

Ofc. L. J. Fennessy, Rochester (New York) Police Dept.

Sgt. William E. Gardner, Richmond (Virginia) Police Dept.

Tech. James J. Garrett, Denver Police Dept.

Master Police Officer Don Palmer, Orlando Police Dept.

Maj. Wilbur W. Williams, Mobile (Alabama) Police Dept.

Lt. David G. Reed, Ogden City (Utah) Police Dept.

Ofc. Dan Mitchell and P. O. Richard H. Krummen, Cincinnati Police Dept.

Sgt. Tom Plehn, Las Vegas Metro Police Dept.

Ofc. Joseph Bonomo, Colorado Springs Police Dept.

Lt. Forrest Billington and Steve Brinkerhoff, San Bernardino County Sheriff's Department, Emergency Vehicle Operations Center

Chief Michael Trevis, Bell (California) Police Dept.

Ofc. Mickey Casey, Charlotte-Mecklenburg (North Carolina) Police Dept.

Capt. John Welter and Lt. Bill Brown, San Diego Police Dept.

Chief Ron Rheam, Anderson (Indiana) Police Dept.

Lt. R. E. Pennington, Tampa Police Dept.

J. Richard Culwell, Tennessee Highway Patrol

Sgt. Ben F. Caperton, Dallas Police Dept.

J. Mathis, Corpus Christi (Texas) Police Dept.

Cpl. Karen Mrowka, Dearborn (Michigan) Police Dept.

Lt. Jeff Grams, Duluth (Minnesota) Police Dept.

Stephen H. McCausland, Maine Dept. of Public Safety

Lt. Geoffrey C. Hunter, Metro Transit Police (Washington, D.C.)

F/Lt. James C. Downer, Michigan State Police

Sgt. William J. Muldoon, Omaha (Nebraska) Police Dept.

Lt. Steve Diamond, Salt Lake City Police Dept.

Major John E. Hershberger, Wichita (Kansas) Police Dept.

Deputy Commissioner D. O. Helmick, California Highway Patrol

Retired Motor Officers:

Legrand Jordan, California Highway Patrol

Sgt. Roderick G. Welsh, Long Beach (California) Police Dept.

John I. Stoner, Salt Lake City Police Dept.

Bob Hale, Los Angeles Police Dept.

Capt. Roy Phillips, Charlotte-Mecklenburg (North Carolina) Police Dept.

George L. Rosemeyer, Pittsburgh Police Dept.

Dick Tush, San Jose Police Dept.

Ken White, Michigan State Police

Today's Motor Officers:

Ofc. Eric Tarr and Ofc. Kelly Harris, Chula Vista (California) Police Dept.

Ofc. Michael Chard, Salt Lake City Police Dept.

Ofc. James Rapata, Chicago Police Dept.

Sgt. Tom Plehn and Ofc. Andrea Smyth, Las Vegas Metro Police Dept.

Ofc. Mike Bissett, Los Angeles Police Dept.

Ofc. Rick Johnson, Hot Springs (Arkansas) Police Dept.

Motorola:

Mary Edith Arnold, Archivist, Motorola Museum of Electronics

Collectors and Restoration Enthusiasts:

John Kelly, Chicago

Michael Kan, Detroit

Dale Walksler, Dale's Harley-Davidson of Mt. Vernon and Wheels Through Time Museum

Stewart "Rev" Monger, Rev's Vintage Rides, Temple City, California

Mike Trompak, Timeless Images Photography, Albuquerque, New Mexico

Michael Daniel Maiello, Parts Manager, Harley's House of Harleys, Oceanside, California

Mark Jahn, San Diego

Mike Fletcher, Editor, Blue Knights News

Sharon Carpenter, Oceanside, California

Civic Historians, Librarians, and Museums:

Patricia E. Heyden, Lansing, Michigan

Barbara Miksicek, St. Louis Police Library

Helen K. Mamalakis, Dearborn, Michigan, Historical Museum

Investigator J.R. (Joe) Schlecter, California Highway Patrol Museum

Leslie Kendall, Petersen Automotive Museum, a branch of the Natural History Museum of Los Angeles County

Sharon Uno, Photo Archivist, Royal Canadian Mounted Police

Ofc. Edward G. Johntree, Historian, Suffolk County Police

Dave Zgola, Pohlman Studios, Incorporated, Milwaukee

An endless, curving stretch of highway pokes its way into the outcropping of a mountain range, marking the edge of the valley. Two motor officers are ahead, riding as a pair, astride powerful Harley-Davidson motorcycles in full police trim. Whether by radio communication, body language, or the instinctive awareness that comes from knowing one another, the officers weave in tandem through traffic lanes with graceful ease. Rolling on the V-twin power and accelerating up and away from other traffic, the motor officers become solitary travelers through the mountain passes in this beautiful country, on this perfect afternoon.

Suddenly, the two spotless helmets look at one another, then find the road again. Within seconds, the helmets let loose with unrestrained and uproarious hoots of laughter, followed by words thrown out against the wind stream, "And they pay us to do this!"

Freedom, adventure, and the chance to be part of an elite team of independent individuals has lured officers onto the seats of police Harleys since the early 1900s. Many had wanted to be motor officers from childhood. One look at an officer on a Harley in a Fourth of July parade was all it took. The personality profile of a mounted officer has changed little over the years. Kids knew that to be a motor officer you had to be strong, smart, alert, daring, disciplined, and in control. It may not have occurred to them that you must also have a sense of humor and the ability to play pranks on your fellow officers. But most of all, you must look cool. Women will swoon, and men will give you a thumbs-up in approval of your chosen means of transportation.

Certainly everyone has had a memorable, personal encounter with a member of the local constabulary. In my case, it was an encounter with a CHP motor officer along one of California's open stretches of freeway. My new black Thunderbird with personalized plates was cruising at 70mph between two packs of traffic. The AC was set, and I was inserting a tape into the cassette player, oblivious to my surroundings and no doubt whistling a happy tune.

Suddenly, I felt the overwhelming presence of another human being in close proximity to my vehicle. I looked to my right and was stunned to see a CHP motor officer right up alongside me, riding a spotless white Harley-Davidson police motorcycle. This officer was huge; he looked as big as a Buick. He just sat there, doing 70mph and staring at me through his sunglasses, an unsmiling mouth shrouded beneath an enormous mustache. I fumbled for the cruise control button, and fell back to the posted speed limit. Without so much as a backward glance, this motor officer was gone. The incident had an effect on me more powerful than any traffic ticket he could have given me. The fact that this guy could appear out of nowhere and stare me down into submission gained him my respect forever.

Motorcycles first replaced horses in law enforcement and often preceded the introduction of four-wheeled motorized vehicles into traffic divisions. Uniforms and equipment essentially went from the back of a horse to the seat of a motorcycle, hence the high boots, breeches, and saddlebags. With the help of motor officers nationwide, we will attempt to trace the history of the Harley-Davidson police motorcycle. In conversation, officers use the term motor synonymously with the words motorcycle, motorbike, or bike. But a motor doesn't enforce the law. The motor is nothing without its mounted officer and the stories he or she tells. And everyone has a story to tell. The fascinating, unpredictable, and risky business of police work is made even more legendary when done from the seat of a Harley.

CHAPTER 1

The Dawn of the Police Motorcycle

Motorcycles began to emerge as a tool of law enforcement, often replacing the horse, as early as 1909. In that year, the city of Pittsburgh converted to its first motorized fleet of Harley-Davidsons. In 1913, the first motorcycles used for law enforcement in Cincinnati were Harley-Davidsons. As a result of their successful use during World War I, motorcycles made the transition to peacetime use with little modification at the factory. The military look of the olive drab paint scheme actually helped to increase sales to both civic and civilian markets. By the mid-twenties, about 3,000 law enforcement and civil service organizations were using Harley-Davidson motorcycles.

During the twenties, motor officers had their work cut out for them. Automobiles had made their way onto American streets in record numbers, and it appeared as though each driver followed his own personal set of guidelines for vehicular operation.

In 1923, the motorcycle squad of the St. Louis (Missouri) Police Department was recognized for its "splendid work capturing speeders" in an article appearing in the St. Louis Police Journal. The squad of about eighteen motors was credited with deterring more crime than any other department on the force. Numbers of arrests increased from about 2,500 in 1921 to around 11,000 in 1922. Much of the increase was attributed to "arrests for failure to stop at boulevards."

The dangers of inclement weather were cited in the journal as having hampered the work of the St. Louis motorcycle squad during the winter of 1922. Rain, snow, and the dangerous, slippery street conditions that come with bad weather were enough to put the officers back into cars for the winter. Exposure to all kinds of weather while on motorcycle duty also resulted

This rather surly looking officer has his ticket writing pencil over his ear, his pad of tickets in his back pocket, and his badge on his belt. He is holding a 1913 "5-35" Harley-Davidson single: a five-horsepower, 35ci four-stroke single-cylinder engine. The lever on the side controls the clutch. The pedals were used to start the motor. If the motor failed, the rider could continue to pedal, with the clutch disengaged, like a standard bicycle. By applying reverse force to the pedals, a standard coaster brake provided stopping power. *Revs Vintage Rides*

in illness among officers, thus reducing the number available for duty.

From the St. Louis Police Journal is a partial list of violations for which "the motorcycle man" was to be on the lookout in 1923: muffler cut open, violation of the Volstead Act, no chauffeur's license, passing a street car discharging passengers, failing to keep to the right-hand curb, parking on the wrong side of the street, driving a business vehicle in a park, suspected of an affray, buying stolen property from a minor, littering the street with

The photo of these two Harleys was shot in Dodge City, Kansas, in the summer of 1915. The 1915 Harleys were the first offered with a headlight option. Both motors appear to have a front wheel-driven speedometer mounted on the handlebars. The motorcycle on the left has a bicycle-type horn on the handlebars. *Revs Vintage Rides*

many speeders seemed to prefer the Forest Park area, the setting for the 1904 St. Louis World's Fair.

An article appearing in the St. Louis Star (August 7, 1904), described problems "the scorchers" caused. Even then, there were drivers who wanted to prove that their gasoline buggy was faster than your gasoline buggy. Although the posted speed limit through the park was 6mph, officers cut drivers some slack until the speeds exceeded 19mph. So the driver who boosted his buggy to 40mph was deserving of a stop.

The Star quotes Capt. McNamee, who declares that "many of the violators of the law are mere boys who are reckless to an alarming degree." Some things never change. In fact, many states had no laws regulating the operation of motor vehicles. It wasn't until 1925 that the state of California, for example, established a minimum age of thirteen for issuance of a driver's license. And even then, it was issued until revoked, without an examination. It's no wonder motor officers had such a difficult time enforcing traffic regulations.

The following is an excerpt from the fall 1971 issue of the St. Louis Police Journal, harking

Even though the date on this photo is 1928, there are three 1929 Harleys in this group, as indicated by their small twin headlights. All but one of the pre-1929 motors in this photo have two additional pursuit lights. Also notice the shape of the officers hats, with and without wires. When the wire is removed, they take on the soft shape of a cap and are less likely to blow off. *Springfield, Missouri, Police Archives*

glass, parking abreast, shooting craps, impersonating an officer, and parking in a safety zone. Speeders, however, continued to present the biggest problem. Known to the department as "scorchers,"

back to the working style of the old-time motor officer who rode during the twenties:

The old motorcycle officer was the Red Baron of the highways and boulevards, the gentleman officer who hunted alone. Most tickets were presented with a skillful monologue, telling the driver that he, an obviously fine man, had made an unfortunate mistake by driving too fast. The officer expressed conviction that this could not possibly happen again in a century. He expressed remorse that he was obliged to ticket such a fine citizen. He stressed the fateful results of care-

A collection of eight motor officers on their 1920 Harleys. Four have sidecars and four are solo models. It is interesting to note the variety of cold weather gear worn by the officers. My favorite is the guy wearing the fedora and his driver with those classy goggles. *Omaha, Nebraska, Police Dept. Archives*

less driving. So well delivered was the monologue that more than one driver felt privileged to receive a ticket from such an excellent officer.

When the Maine State Police was founded in 1925, the first forty troopers were issued a gun, a law book, and a Harley-Davidson motorcycle. They were told to enforce the law, earning a salary of $25 per week. The motorcycle troopers patrolled the state's highways, in which there was only one paved road. During the winter months, the troopers rode horses on patrol, because two-wheeled motorcycles were impossible to ride safely in the snow. In cold weather, motor officers were known to stuff rolled up newspapers inside their pants legs in an effort to keep warm.

Riding a motorcycle was dangerous work. Three Maine State troopers were killed in motorcycle accidents in the first three years. Others had frequent spills on Maine's unpaved roads or in collisions with Model T's. Capt. Eddie Marks, who served the Maine State Police from 1925 to 1975, was reputed to have patrolled the state on his motorcycle with his black bear, "Minnie," seated in a sidecar. The Maine State Police began to phase out motorcycles in 1936 in favor of patrol cars. By the end of the forties, all of the Harley-Davidsons had been sold off at public auction, and the department never returned to the two-wheeled vehicles.

In California, traffic enforcement began at the local level. The first known traffic officer in California was M. F. "Mike" Brown, who operated out of San Mateo County, south of San Francisco, beginning in 1911. Other counties followed suit. Officers were often political appointees who had to furnish their own motorcycles. The county government picked up the tab for vehicle maintenance. Local merchants often provided tires and gasoline in exchange for advertising. While patrolling, motor officers looked

In the twenties, the Omaha Police Department had a unique idea for a rapid response police force. They invented the "pill box" outpost, a simple concept of placing two officers with a sidecar-equipped motor in a garage-like structure. Their pill box had a telephone connected to headquarters. Upon receiving a call from dispatch, they mounted their trusty Harley and rushed to the scene of the crime. If I were the driver of this motor, I would ask my partner to point his rifle in another direction. *Omaha, Nebraska, Police Dept. Archives*

for red flags displayed at a service station or store. The flag was the signal for the officers to call headquarters for a message. Early uniforms were simply those worn by military officers.

In 1919, the Charlotte (North Carolina) Police Department hired its first two motorcycle officers, Fred Staton and J. Paxton, who rode Harleys on patrol. In 1929, the motorcycle fleet of the Cincinnati Police Department included ten Indians, seven Hendersons, and sixteen Harley-Davidsons. By the mid-twenties, over 1,400 police and sheriff's departments were riding Harley-Davidson motorcycles on patrol. At the close of the decade, the number increased to 2,900.

The California Highway Patrol; was officially established via legislation in 1929 although the group, known as the California Association of Highway Patrolmen, had been in existence since 1920. The department began with 280 uniformed men, eighty patrol vehicles, and 225 motorcycles. Communication from the field to local headquarters became standardized. The standard policy included officers out on patrol to phone their offices each hour for messages. They relied upon passing motorists to report injuries, fatalities, or requests for assistance. It wasn't until 1933 that Harley-Davidson was designated as the official CHP motorcycle statewide.

With what we know about today's motorcycles, it is interesting to go back to these very early days and imagine riding one of those models to

This circa 1920 early twin was assigned to the Rochester Police Department. Barely visible on the tank in front of the Harley-Davidson logo are the initials "R.P.D." *Rochester, New York, Police Archives*

Officer Carl Bohnet on his 1928 Harley twin. Prior to the official formation of the CHP in 1929, officers were members of the California Association of Highway Patrolmen (CAHP). The color of the motorcycle was olive green with maroon striping, including a gold center stripe. *California Highway Patrol Archives*

enforce the law. The first twin used for police work in 1909 had only 7hp. It had no suspension, electronics, or lights. In 1912, Harley-Davidson introduced a motorcycle clutch, although the bicycle-type pedals were still connected to allow the rider to get the motor started by pedaling away. The step-starter was introduced in 1914, eliminating the need to pedal or run alongside the motorcycle to get it going. In about 1915, motor officers could get an 11hp model with a headlight, taillight, and

horn. The first sidecar was introduced in 1915. An electrical system was first offered on the 20J V-twin model in 1920, and a speedometer was offered as an option. And later, in about 1923, a front stand appeared. Innovations for 1925 included a drop-forged steel frame, a carburetor air-cleaner, and a new tear-drop gas tank. And of course, in 1929, the Big Twin Flathead emerged. This model 45 had a vertical starter and double headlight. With each new innovation or improvement, the motorcycle became a better tool for the motor officer.

During these early years, police agencies purchased motorcycles not much different from those offered to the civilian riding public. There were few options to order from the factory, and certainly nothing that could be associated with police work. Police agencies and the motor officers themselves were often responsible for adding any extras. Beginning in the early thirties, police options started to show up on the order forms, and the list continued to grow throughout the years.

V-Twin Tales: Harleys on Patrol

Motor Officer George E. "Ed" VanWagenen
Sergeant Les Langford wrote an article that appeared in the Utah Trooper about Patrolman George E. "Ed" VanWagenen. Born in 1888, Ed rode for the *Utah Highway* Patrol from about 1927 until his death in the line of duty in 1931. What follows is an excerpt from Sgt. Langford's article.

At the time he was hired by the Utah Highway Patrol, Ed VanWagenen was 39 years

About the time of this photo (circa 1924), the number of California's vehicle registrations exceeded one million. These officers are members of the California Association of Highway Patrolmen (CAHP), the forerunner of today's California Highway Patrol. All officers are wearing cross-draw gun holsters and unique caps. *California Highway Patrol Archives*

California Highway Patrol Officer Jim Lane sits on a 1925 model 74 Harley. Two items of note include the modified exhaust with the bologna-sliced muffler, and the horn, relocated to the fender. *California Highway Patrol Archives*

A 1925 portrait of the Maine State Police. It is odd to see the Harleys on the porch and the chairs on the ground. *Maine State Police*

RIGHT
The exact details of this photo are unknown. It is believed to be a mid-twenties Harley. The armor plating has been added, making this an effective urban assault vehicle. A large bulletproof glass panel has been added in front of the driver so he can lean forward and be protected yet still see where he is going. The sidecar passenger has gun ports and small, bulletproof windows. *Harley-Davidson Archives*

This 1923 Harley-Davidson was painted olive drab with three gold pinstripes and powered by a 74ci twin. The left side of the handlebar has an accessory light. *Orlando, Florida, Police Archives*

of age, and his five children ranged in age from 5 to 13. As a three-year veteran with the Provo Police Department, he had much to offer the Utah Highway Patrol. His area of assignment included all of Utah County. All travel outside Provo city limits was on gravel and dirt roads. Although Ed was excited for the opportunity to patrol such a vast area, he realized that there was no backup on these remote sections of road. With no communications and the passing of only an occasional motorist, patrolmen learned to solve a variety of problems. Being a peace maker, politician, doctor, nurse, mechanic, tour guide, marriage counselor, and big brother were all duties required of patrolmen.

The first Utah Highway Patrolmen were issued 1927 Harley-Davidson motorcycles with a side

shift lever and foot clutch. Black, knee-high boots were also issued equipment, which, besides being attractive, protected the officers' legs from the heat and flying oil of the motorcycle engines (these early Harleys had exposed pushrods and valve rocker arms). It was necessary to use boot hooks to get the boots on and a boot jack to get them off.

With fewer than 50 miles of paved roads in the entire state, most speed limits were limited to 35 to 40 miles per hour on gravel roads, outside of urban areas. High speed chases of 55 to 60mph were really flying on these twisting, narrow, gravel roads. This new breed of police officer spent many hours on their Harley-Davidsons, much like the lawmen of the 1800s who spent time on their horses.

Shortly after joining the Patrol, Ed VanWagenen was on routine patrol on Canyon Road near Provo, Utah. Upon rounding a sharp curve, he discovered a vehicle being driven on the wrong side of the road, headed directly toward him. Instinctively, Patrolman VanWagenen swerved to the right to avoid a head-on collision. Running off the

Prior to the introduction of the Servi-Car, this was the way officers marked tires. The sidecar offered the stability for this low-speed task, at the expense of two officers.
Harley-Davidson Archives

right side of the road, he went down an embankment and through a barbed wire fence. The left handlebar of his Harley struck a fence post, cutting off the index finger of his left hand. The vehicle that caused this accident failed to stop. Patrolman VanWagenen dragged his damaged Harley-Davidson back onto the graveled road, retrieved the finger from the barrow pit, and drove himself to the Aird Hospital. Doctors attempted to graft the finger back to his hand, but the operation was not successful. Despite this serious injury, Ed never told his children. Three or four months later, one of the children noticed the missing finger and learned of his father's experience.

The three motorcycles on the right are Harleys with the balance of the line-up Indians. This photo is typical of unit portraits in the late twenties; all the motors were lined up with their lieutenant and the chief of police outside the station. *Omaha, Nebraska, Police Dept. Archives*

Two police Harleys, a 1928 on the left and a 1929 on the right. The 1928 has the "Police" plate on the front fender, twin pursuit lights, and speedometer. Both motorcycles were finished in olive green with maroon striping. The horizontally mounted circular container below the headlight is a tool kit. Notice the officers' hats. The officer on the left has removed the wire from his hat, giving it a floppy look. The officer on the right has kept the wire installed for proper blocking. These wires were often removed to reduce the incidence of high-speed hat loss due to airflow hitting the large, flat surface of the hat. *Springfield, Missouri, Police Archives*

RIGHT
Officers from four different departments have stopped by to visit their local Harley dealer. All are riding 1928 or earlier Harley-Davidson motorcycles with sidecars. The variety and styles of uniforms are very interesting.

CHAPTER 2

The Thirties: A Dangerous Time

During the thirties, traffic fatalities were increasing at an alarming rate. Many cities felt that if left unchecked, speeding and failure to observe traffic regulations would continue to result in more accidents and fatalities. The introduction of motorcycle squads was looked to as a solution to this problem. By virtue of their presence and maneuverability, motor officers in many cities were credited with a reduction in the number of accidents and fatalities wherever they patrolled.

In 1930, there were over 3,000 police agencies using Harley-Davidson motorcycles. Among the many law enforcement agencies riding Harleys, the following departments were featured in the 1935 issue of the *The Enthusiast*: St. Paul Park Police, Kalamazoo Police, Minnesota Highway Patrol, Sewickley (Pennsylvania) Police, Beaumont (Texas) Police, Atkinson (Wisconsin) Police, San Antonio (Texas) Police, Cleveland (Ohio) Police, Syracuse (New York) Police, Palm Beach (Florida) Police, Hillsborough County (Florida) Patrol, Detroit Police, Milwaukee Police, Mount Kisco (New York) Police, Ridgewood (New Jersey) Police, New Jersey State Police, Washington State Patrol, Denver Police, California Highway Patrol, and the New York State Police.

Then, as today, Harley-Davidson police motorcycles were also sold to law enforcement agencies in foreign countries. In 1935, Harleys were used by the Shanghai French Municipal Council (China); the Rotterdam (Holland) Police for escort, patrol, and pursuit; the Motorcycle Corps of the Customs Guards in Cúcuta, Colom-

This 1930 California Highway Patrol twin was painted white with gold striping. Between the dual headlights rests a single pursuit light. On the front frame is a small bicycle-type tire pump. The officer carries a .45 caliber automatic pistol in a military style holster instead of the usual .38 police special revolver. *California Highway Patrol Archives*

bia (South America); and the harbor patrol in Montreal, Canada.

Innovations and Police Options

The 1930 model introduced some improvements that could be considered benefits for motor officers: larger front and rear brakes, larger tires, and a built-in front fork lock. The 1930 motorcycle order form has the first indication of a police option: the Police Special Speedometer. In 1931, a front wheel siren, first-aid kit, and Pyrene fire extinguisher were offered for the first time as options on the order form. The Servi-Car

Fifteen brand-new 1930 Harleys of the Milwaukee County Police Squad. Harley offered two twins in 1930. These are equipped with the 74ci motor that had a shaky beginning. Highly touted upon its 1930 introduction, the 74ci was plagued with problems that were quickly resolved. *Harley-Davidson Archives*

was introduced in late 1931 for the 1932 model year. Intended primarily for commercial use, police departments realized this handy little vehicle could also be used to enforce parking regulations and for traffic control.

In 1931, Harley-Davidson introduced the new Burgess Muffler, featuring a gas-deflecting muffler end that directed the exhaust downward into the airstream instead of allowing it to swirl upward, collecting in the sidecar and handlebar windshield. Other small improvements included larger gas filler caps, crank pins made of a stronger grade of steel, and mufflers and exhaust pipes made from heat-resistant enamel. Another improvement was the relocation of the toolbox from the front fork, allowing for a neater horn mounting.

I'm sure this RCMP officer looked great on his 1930 Harley. The exaggerated jodhpurs and the red tunic made for a stunning uniform. Sidecars were quite popular in the colder climates as they could be used year-round. *RCMP Archives*

Two officers of the California Highway Patrol ride down the street on their 1930 model 74 motors. The cylinder under the headlights is the tool kit. The cylinder on the rear luggage rack is a first-aid kit. *California Highway Patrol Archives*

According to information found in the Petersen Automotive Museum in Los Angeles, older model police motorcycles could be updated at the factory. On display at the museum is a 1932 Harley-Davidson that was factory updated to 1934 specifications. When the police department wanted its fleet modernized, they sent the motorcycles back to the factory for updating, thereby giving them the appearance of a new motorcycle for a fraction of the cost. Practices like this often cause confusion and disagreement among collectors and restoration enthusiasts.

On the 1934 Season Order Blank, we see for the first time, under special equipment, the following options associated with police use: safety guards and pursuit lamps (please specify "Little King" or "Little Beauty").

In 1935, ordering of special options was simplified by dividing them into equipment groups. Police Group No.1 included the following options packaged as a group: safety guard, jiffy stand, 100 mile maximum hand-lighted speedometer, and a rear wheel siren. The Deluxe Police Group included everything in Police

Group No. 1 plus: steering damper, ride control, stop light, luggage carrier, first-aid kit, Pyrene fire extinguisher, and Little Beauty pursuit lights. An additional "a la carte" Police option list included a radio receiving set (please specify wave length).

The February 1935 police issue of *The Enthusiast* described the various improvements in the 1935 police model. In the area of safety, the manufacturer described improved handling, improved brakes, and better visibility at night. The 1935 police model was improved by a change in toolbox location. By removing the toolbox from the front fork and fitting it to the right side of the frame, the weight on the front fork was reduced. According to the manufacturer, moving the toolbox gave the motorcycle a "lighter feel." The large, internal, expanding brakes on the 1935 model were improved to give longer life and better performance by using harder brake linings

August 1937 Harley advertisement touts the effectiveness of radio-equipped Harleys. With a careful look at the small inset photo at the bottom, you will notice that it looks very similar to the large photo in the October 1937 ad. It was not unusual for the art department to do a little creative work to update a file photo. *Harley-Davidson Archives*

This special constable from the town of Huntington, New York, seems quite proud of the trophy he is holding. He could have easily won it for the cleanliness of his 1931 74 twin. The standard color for 1931 was olive green, but this motor is white with a standard Harley-Davidson tank logo and striping. *Suffolk County Police Museum*

and carburized brake drums. A more important feature, however, according to the manufacturer, was the adjustable brake shoe pivot stud on which the brake shoes "hinge." By adjusting and tightening the stud nut with the brakes applied, the stud was locked in the correct spot for full brake efficiency.

Another safety feature cited by Harley-Davidson on the 1935 model was the color known as Safety Silver, featured in 1934 for the police model and retained in 1935 as the standard police color. The reflective nature of the paint made the motorcycle more visible at night. In addition, the 1935 model featured a new bee-hive taillight lens. Because of its shape, it was vis-

ible to drivers of other vehicles from either side as well as from the rear. Also touted as a new safety feature for 1935 was the prefocused headlight. The prefocused bulb, when placed in the lamp, had its filaments located in proper relation to the lens and reflector. The beam was therefore concentrated on the road ahead, giving the rider greater visibility and a clean beam of light.

According to the issue of *The Enthusiast*, Harley-Davidson engineers improved engine performance of the 1935 police model, which had to contend with an increasing number of powerful automobiles on the roads. "The amazing snap and acceleration" of the 1935 motors was due to the use of cam-ground T-slot pistons in conjunction with honed, mirror-finish cylinders.

Although silver and black were the colors recommended for police use, five additional color combinations were available in 1935 at no extra charge: Teak Red and Black, Olive Green and Black, Verdant Green and Black, Venetian Blue

Pictured here on his 1930 model 74 is Motor Officer Frank Pike. He was slightly wounded in the infamous "Young Brothers Massacre," on January 2, 1932. This motorcycle has an additional large headlight between the standard twin headlights. On the motorcycle's frame just to the left of the officer's right hand is the siren, in an unusual high mount. The siren is actuated by the lever at the rear of the right floorboard. Officer Pike takes great pride in his appearance. His boots are highly polished, and his revolver is pulled around to the front to better display the pearl handle for the photo. The wheel patch on his sleeve is unusual, as most motor units have the winged wheel or the winged wheel pierced with an arrow. The circumstances of this photo, which appears to have been taken in someone's kitchen, remain a mystery! *Springfield, Missouri, Police Archives*

and Silver, and Egyptian Ivory and Brown. The second color in each combination appears on the tank panels and sides of the fenders. Base parts (such as frames, forks, chain guards, rims, and hubs) were painted black.

In 1936, the 61ci EL model, which was later dubbed the "Knucklehead," was introduced. This more powerful motor enabled the Harley police motorcycle to compete more effectively with the Indian and the automobile. A reverse gear was an option for those who ran sidecars. The Deluxe Police Group consisted of the following options: siren, speedometer with hand stop, luggage rack, first-aid kit, fire extinguisher, and pursuit lights. If you ordered the standard Police Group, you received a rear wheel siren and speedometer. Beginning in 1939, more and more departments were ordering Police Combinations, which consisted

of a three-speed transmission, medium compression motor, and medium gearing for police work in city service or congested traffic areas, offered at no additional charge.

Police Duty: Traffic

The 1930 edition of the annual Springfield (Missouri) Police Department Yearbook discussed the efforts and value of what was called the Motor Cycle Division:

"The motorcycle division of the Springfield Police Department, since its inception, has proved to be a valuable and necessary asset. The personnel of this division is made up of eight alert and clean-cut young men. Young men in years, but in the performance of their duties, they conduct themselves like veterans. These men patrol the city's streets day and night. Four riding day and four at night on their motorcy-

Harley police ads in the thirties incorporated as many current customers as possible. Images of satisfied customers boosted the prospective buyers' confidence in the product and their belief that many departments were riding Harleys. I love the hat on Trooper Joe Hunt. Do you think he fixed it that way or did it take a set from the wind as he rode? *Harley-Davidson Archives*

Officer Waidie Phillips of the Springfield Police Department astride his 1930 Model 74. The headlight configuration is unique for a 1930 Harley. But the dual exhaust pipes are distinctive of a 1930 model. This motorcycle also has front and rear stands, a fire extinguisher, and a rear wheel siren. *Springfield, Missouri, Police Archives*

cles. One man is nearly always kept stationed at headquarters to answer emergency calls. They regulate traffic and their presence on the streets helps keep down the number of automobile accidents because of their efficient and rigid prosecution of speeders and reckless drivers who menace life and property on the city's streets. They are always courteous and considerate, but take their duties seriously.

The motorcycle officer's job is dangerous. In addition to the normal risk he runs as a police officer in dealing with law breakers, he is in constant danger of breaking a limb or being killed from a spill on his machine. For the motorcycle officer must often ride at great speed, regardless of the condition of the traffic or the street, slippery and wet with rain or snow or ice."

As the nation recovered from the depression, life in the cities began to change. For one thing, more and more automobiles were now competing for use of the streets. Many cities didn't anticipate the consequences of unregulated traffic. In her book, *Behind the Badge: The History of the Lansing Police Department*, historian Patricia Heyden writes that the city of Lansing, Michigan, didn't even have a Traffic Commission until 1932. With rivers, bridges, and railroads all converging in the central city, new ordinances to regulate pedestrian and vehicular traffic were urgently needed. It was at this time that the Traffic Division was expanded to include six motorcycles, both Harley-Davidsons and Indians. They were responsible for directing traffic at congested intersections. Among these motor officers were those designated as Minutemen. A Minuteman was assigned to assist the desk command officer at headquarters. If an emergency call came in, the Minuteman was sent out to the scene on his motorcycle, offering a quick response to the caller in need.

During the thirties, the Michigan State Police used the big Harley-Davidson motorcycle. Although the motorcycle could achieve high speeds by the standards of the day, technology governing the rest of the vehicle did not keep pace. Motorcycles of the day generally had inadequate mechanical drum brakes, no suspension system to speak of, and rode on crude tires. The highways themselves did not make riding a motorcycle any easier or safer. A large portion of the state trunk line highway of Michigan was still gravel. Paved portions were often badly crowned and narrow. Many paved intersections were fed by at least one gravel road, thus resulting in gravel on the pavement. Most road conditions were inherently dangerous to motorcycle riding. Troopers were at additional risk with no helmets, windshields, or fairings.

By the late thirties, the function of the Michigan State Police changed and expanded. Their primary focus shifted to rural areas of the state and to the use of the patrol car. During the winter of 1941–1942, all motorcycles were sold. The Michigan State Police did not officially climb back onto Harleys until June 1, 1994.

In 1933, the Harley-Davidson motorcycle was designated as the official motorcycle for the California Highway Patrol. The purchase of fifty-five 1935 Harley-Davidson police motorcycles brought the total number of motors in use by the CHP to 437. All CHP motorcycles were painted white, and each one was optioned as follows (according to the February 1935 issue of *The Enthusiast*): first-aid kit, fire-fighting equipment, flashlight, red and white pursuit lights, safety guard, windshield, jiffy stand, stop light, siren, and memo pad holder. In 1936, construction of experimental motorcycle radio receivers began. It wasn't until 1938, however, that the CHP bought its first radio receiver (low-power, AM-band) from RCA for installation on patrol motorcycles.

The Salt Lake City Police Department Motorcycle Drill Team during the mid-thirties. All rode Harleys. *Salt Lake City, Utah, Police Archives*

In 1935, the Cincinnati Police Department purchased fifteen new motorcycles, bringing their total to thirty-five. Ten of those were Harleys. One-way radios that could receive only were installed on the six Harleys with sidecars. The entire motorcycle fleet was valued at about $6,800. The first Cincinnati police officer to be killed on duty while riding a motor was Patrolman J. Roy Hicks, whose fatal accident occurred on February 25, 1935. Throughout the remainder of the thirties,

Cincinnati's fleet of motorcycles stayed at about forty, including solo motorcycles, Servi-Cars, and sidecar rigs.

Uniforms

To illustrate what well-dressed motor officers were wearing during this era, we'll describe the uniform of the Springfield, Missouri, motor squad as they were dressed in a 1930 photo: The uniform consisted of knee-high leather boots, jodhpur style breeches, thigh-length coat with breast and hip pockets, John Browne leather belt and sash, gun holster positioned for a right-hand cross draw, white shirt, black bow tie, and soft cap tilted slightly off to one side.

V-Twin Tales: Harleys on Patrol

Motor Officer Legrand Jordan

Legrand Jordan rode for the Los Angeles County Motor Patrol from 1930 to 1932, and for the CHP until his disability retirement in 1956, due to back injuries from years on the motorcycle. (Although the CHP was established in 1929, Los Angeles County held out until 1932 before officially becoming part of the CHP.) Jordan designed his own motorcycle in 1932, applied for a patent, and received one in 1937. The Jordan Motorcycle is on display at the Petersen Automotive Museum in Los Angeles.

In those very early days, no training for motor officers was offered. In fact, officers had to prove they could ride a motorcycle when they took the examination. All the boys on the motor squad had experience on motorcycles, including Jordan, who had been riding since 1917. When he applied with the Los Angeles County Motor Patrol, he didn't think they would take him because he was so skinny; his weight fell to just within the guidelines of the physical requirements. Indeed, he was the thinnest man on the squad.

One day when his sergeant was first showing him the ropes, the sergeant asked Jordan, "Hey, Slim, you like ice cream?" It turned out an ice cream factory operated in the neighborhood, and the foreman invited Jordan to stop by for ice cream anytime. Jordan ate two quarts

The New Mexico Motor Patrol's 1934 Harleys were silver with teak red trim and sported 1934 Harley-Davidson tank graphics modified by adding the initials "NMMP" inside the diamond. The word "Police" is lettered on the front fender. Originally formed in 1931, the New Mexico Motor Patrol changed its name in 1935 to the New Mexico State Police. Their use of motorcycles ended in the late forties. *New Mexico State Police Association*

of ice cream a day for a month, hoping it would put some weight on him, but it never did.

One of the problems with the Harleys was the tendency of the motorcycle to backfire. Firing both spark plugs at the same time put a spark in the front cylinder while the intake valve was open. There was an air intake valve on the left side that pointed to the back. Many times, Officer Jordan saw fire come out of that tube.

New Mexico Motor Patrol officers in dress uniforms with new 1934 Harley motorcycles. *New Mexico State Police Association*

Some motorcycles caught fire and burned up; on many more, the saddle caught fire.

The weapon Jordan carried was an old-style revolver. He objected to this weapon because, he recalled, it was the same type used by the pioneers a hundred years ago. For a long time, the CHP leadership was reluctant to switch to automatic weapons. Jordan remembers the night he chased a stolen car twenty-one miles, wide open on the Harley. The motor had just been in for a tune-up, but he could only do 75mph. The Ford he was chasing could do 85mph. When the car got into traffic, the Harley caught up, but then the Ford would get out in the open and leave the Harley behind. Finally, Jordan caught up to the driver, but he had spent all six rounds shooting at the car during the pursuit.

"When this guy got out of his car with his hands up," recalled Jordan, "I was holding an empty gun on him! So I was awful glad he couldn't count to six." Had the weapon been an automatic, said Jordan, "you could slap in another clip while you're going."

Firing a weapon during a pursuit was difficult, especially with a right-hand throttle.

When the CHP was first founded, officers rode both Hendersons and Harley-Davidsons, and had them all changed to a left-hand throttle so that a right-handed man could draw his weapon while riding. Eventually, the patrol discontinued the left-hand throttle. One of the city officers rigged up a foot throttle. "But," recalled Jordan, "that Harley shook so bad, it didn't do him much good."

Jordan was lucky to have had very few mishaps with the motorcycle. On one occasion, he was chasing a speeder when a driver pulled right in front of him. He broadsided the car, went over the handlebars, and cut his scalp. He was off work for only two weeks.

He didn't chase speeders very often, however. "The ignition on the Harley," Jordan explained, "was such that you never knew how many times you'd have to kick it to get started. Often, you'd have to kick it half a dozen times to get it going, and by that time, your speeder was out of sight. If that Harley wouldn't start on the first kick, I'd just let them go." Instead, Jordan cited drivers for mechanical offenses, such as bad brakes. A trained mechanic, Jordan could observe driver and vehicle behavior that others might overlook. He would sit at a corner and watch vehicles as they approached the stop sign. If the driver started pulling on the handbrake, Jordan knew it was because he had no foot brake. Officer Jordan wrote more tickets for bad brakes than the rest of his squad put together.

When Harley-Davidson finally came out with the Hydra-Glide hydraulic fork design in 1949, Jordan got one of them for police duty. He was due for a new machine, so he went down to the dealership to take delivery of his new motor. As soon as he took it out on the road, oil began spraying out from the bottom of the forks, soaking his pants. He went back to the dealer, and, according to Jordan, they "put some little, bitty valves at the top of these forks." This stopped the oil from coming out the bottom, but by the end of the shift the next day, his shirt front was covered in oil. All of those machines were recalled and redesigned.

The Harley engineers also made a change in the carburetor that year, but it made

RIGHT
Harley had it right in this ad; speeders did slow down when they saw a motorcycle officer. It's still true today! *Harley-Davidson Archives*

26

Reckless Speeders

—SLOW DOWN WHEN THEY SEE MOTORCYCLE OFFICERS

There is no longer any doubt about the outstanding value of having uniformed officers on motorcycles patrolling streets and highways day and night. Reduction of accidents and violations has proved to more and more enforcement departments that this method "puts the brakes" on recklessness and speeding. Why? Because motorcycles keep the officers where they can be seen—where their presence makes would-be violators unwilling to "take chances." All the more reason for mounting YOUR squads on 1937 Harley-Davidson Police Motorcycles, whose many improvements make them the ideal vehicles for fast, dependable, low-cost police service. . . . . . Phone your nearby Harley-Davidson Dealer NOW—to bring over a new 1937 model for your inspection. Or write us for literature.

Harley-Davidson Motor Co.   *Dept. PU*   Milwaukee, Wis.

Capt. R. A. Schmoke of the California Highway Patrol—in command of the detail of 39 Harley-Davidsons —keeping traffic in hand day and night on the great San Francisco-Oakland Bay bridge.

HARLEY-DAVIDSON
The Police Motorcycle

SAFETY POSTER Free!

A striking safety poster that has gained nation-wide recognition and approval. Copies free to Enforcement Departments on request. Write promptly as supply is limited.

The 1934 Harleys had a new rear fender with a graceful curving rear edge. The taillight was redesigned to be more streamlined. Both of these modifications fit the style of the day, as design trends were moving from Art Deco to streamlined.

the bikes hard to start. Jordan recalled one particular day when he needed to fill up the tank at a gas station. It took fifty-four kicks to get the motor started to ride to the gas station, and then another forty kicks (counted and witnessed by the gas station manager) to get it started for the return trip.

Motor Officer Frank Pike

Motor officer Frank Pike, Chief of Police for the Springfield (Missouri) Police Department, was slightly wounded in the infamous "Young Brothers Massacre" that occurred in Springfield on January 2, 1932. According to some, this event still holds the title of most law enforcement officers (six) killed at one time in the history of the United States. Officer Pike was one of only three survivors of the massacre.

Officers had driven to the home of the two Young brothers to make an arrest for a stolen auto and the murder of a city marshal. Whey they arrived, a gun battle ensued, and the Young brothers escaped. They were later surrounded in Houston, Texas, and found dead from suicide. The department has had inquiries over the years about this incident with talk of making a movie, but footage has yet to be shot.

Motor Officer Ken White

Ken White rode Harley-Davidson motorcycles for the Michigan State Police, beginning in 1929. Here is his V-Twin Tale, entitled "Motorcycles and Me."

Seeing the troops back on motorcycles again brings back old memories—about sixty-four year's worth. It was in April 1929 that I first climbed astride an old Harley. We were on the old parade grounds next to Mapes Hall in East Lansing. This was hallowed ground. A decade earlier another group of men learned to ride horses on this same soil.

I had now reached the pinnacle of my dreams. I was actually going to ride a motor-

Chrome shifter and carb intake grace this 1934 model 74. The California Highway Patrol placed its logo on the side of the tank. A looped oil line runs from the bottom of the tank. This loop is designed to absorb the vibration of the motor.

The right floorboard on this 1934 CHP motor has the Harley-Davidson logo molded into its hard rubber covering. The CHP specified cadmium plating on brake and clutch pedals (shown). The black lever at the rear of the floorboard is for the siren.

cycle. Throughout my teenage years, I had wanted to own a motorcycle. But my Dad had two standard excuses why I couldn't. First, he couldn't afford it, and second, I might kill myself on one! Little did I know that I would spend the better part of the next eleven summers on one. How could I have imagined that it would be as hard to get off the thing as it was to get on.

We had the most unforgiving instructor. Chuck Wyans felt that every man should be a born motorcycle rider. (It took me a week of just coasting down a ramp off the barn floor on a bicycle, before I could get the knack of pedaling without tipping over). After a few days of riding around the parade ground at 10mph in low gear, we were ready for the big time. Chuck took us out on the road to a location where the county had just laid about a mile of loose gravel. I think he conspired to have it laid just for us! He gathered us around him and explained that the way to go through loose gravel was to give it lots of gas. I was in the back of the pack next to a fellow who owned a bike. He said not to heed the instructor, but to go slow and sort of walk it through with your feet on the ground, if need be. By the time we all regrouped at the other end, most everyone had spilled, tearing their clothes and scraping their hands in the process. My buddy and I didn't have a scratch. But Chuck bawled us out for not keeping up.

I learned a bit of good advice from Chuck. He said that as long as we respected the machine, we would have no trouble. But if we ever got to think that we knew more than the machine— watch out. You learned mostly by doing. I learned the hard way. Never pass a slow moving car if there is a driveway or intersection just ahead. I tried that, and the car started to turn left onto a gravel side road. Although I missed colliding with the car, I upset the bike, tore my uniform, and got a few scratches. When I went back to the post to change, the first thing the sergeant asked about was the condition of the bike. I know of two troopers who were not so fortunate. Adrian Locker and Leon Hopkins both lost legs by trying to pass a car as it made a left turn. Now that we have directional turn signals on vehicles, this danger has been diminished to some extent.

In addition to the basic training of how to ride the machine, we also were shown how to mend a broken chain and how to take off the wheels in case of a flat. This was not much different than repairing a bicycle. There was a small tool-

This restored 1934 model 74 conforms to California Highway Patrol specs. Retired from patrolling California's freeways, it now rests in the beautiful Petersen Automotive Museum in Los Angeles.

RIGHT
The rear wheel siren on this 1934 Harley is foot-actuated by a lever at the rear of the right floorboard. The officer depressed it with the heel of his boot when he needed to sound it. The linkage rotated the siren's knurled shaft into the tire; it spun, creating the siren wail as we know it. If kept depressed, the siren reached an extremely high frequency. To keep a varied pitch, the officer had to modulate the pedal. And, oh yes, this was done while in high-speed pursuit. The rear fender valence on this 74ci was modified for the siren drive. In typical Harley fashion, they radiused the edge of the valence for a stylish transition.

box on the front fork that carried the necessary tools and spare chain links. We all dreaded getting a flat tire. There was nothing you could do but remove the wheel, get a ride from a passing car to a gas station, and then get a ride back. If there was a sheriff or city policeman around, you could call them for a ride.

I think I have covered most of lower Michigan on a motorcycle. I rode out of White Pigeon, Paw Paw, Reed City, Wayne, Bay City, Grand Haven, and Alpena. I rode out of White Pigeon and Paw Paw when they were the only two posts in southwest Michigan. Somebody got the bright idea of what they called a Loop Patrol. You left White Pigeon in the morning, going west via Cassopolic Harbor and staying overnight in Paw Paw. At the same time, another trooper was leaving Paw Paw, going east to

Sneaking a peak around the billboard is a CHP officer watching me photograph his motor. This beautifully restored 1934 model 74 is finished, as specified by the CHP, in white with gold pinstriping.

In 1934, this special 100mph police speedometer was a $36 option. The speedometer was driven off the rear sprocket. Chrome caps on the tank are for oil (left) and gas (right).

Kazoo, Augusta, and Battle Creek down to Coldwater and west to White Pigeon, which you covered the next day.

My New Buffalo run could have been a moneymaker for me. We picked up a lot of speeders coming into New Buffalo from Chicago. They all wanted to hand you a five or a ten.

RIGHT
The California Highway Patrol specified an upright cylindrical first-aid kit. The cylinder was made of aluminum and lacked durability. Alongside is the Pyrene fire extinguisher.

The Michigan State Police used these model 74s in the early thirties. *Michigan State Police Archives*

I took them into the local JP, where he offered me a dollar. The JP also kept a gallon of wine under his desk and offered to treat me. I told him no. If I wanted remuneration, I could make more money out on the road from the speeders!

They only ran that type of patrol for about a month or so in the summer of 1929. We were supposed to stop at small towns, look up the JP, and work traffic for speeders. While there was no speed limit on state roads in rural areas, there were speed limits in towns. Every town had a problem with speeders, so we were there to make our presence felt. Every small town loved us. There were few private motorcycles on the road, so we were very visible. If you saw a motorcycle on the road, chances were ninety-nine to one it was a trooper. We could park on the edge of town for a half hour, and slow traffic to a walk.

We were big on showcasing ourselves in those days. Chances were good that if there was a public gathering of any size, there would be a few troopers on hand on motorcycles. Headquarters didn't miss an opportunity to get those machines and men where they could be seen. The trooper on a bike was the only visible means of displaying ourselves in those early days. It was not until later years that marked cars became readily identifiable.

Duty on a motorcycle wasn't all fun and games. I find it rather ironic that most of the violence to our men on bikes took place in the very area of my first post, White Pigeon. Cpl. Mapes was killed by a rum runner near Sturgis. Trooper Burke was killed north of Sturgis by bank robbers. Trooper Nelson was assaulted by bandits near Jonesville and would have been killed had it not been for the intervention of a truck driver. All these men were alone on a bike. I am amused today when I hear about the danger of one-man patrols, what with two-way radios, computers, and the availability of backup. They should have ridden bikes sixty years ago!

In the mid-thirties, we had one-way radios on the bikes in lower Michigan. You had to

be within one hundred miles of the transmitter, of which we had three: Lansing, Paw Paw, and Houghton Lake. The radio would emit a long tone signal, indicating that a message was forthcoming. When you heard this, you pulled off the road, turned off the engine, turned up the volume, and waited for the message. If conditions were ideal, you might be able to hear it. Each message was repeated three times within a fifteen minute period. But the post never knew if you actually received or heard the message or not. If it was something serious, you had to hunt down a phone and call the post.

As cars became faster and roads better, the bike began to lose some of its importance. In 1929, a bike could run about 80mph. The average car had a top speed of 65 to 70mph, but the highway conditions would generally not permit those speeds. When I worked US 112, there were several curves where top speed was about 30mph. Bikes

BELOW
This 1934 Ford V-8 was fast, but not fast enough to outrun a well-tuned 74ci Harley and an experienced Michigan State Police trooper. On the luggage carrier of this 1934 solo is the large receive-only radio. Saddlebags on either side of the rear wheel and a handlebar-mounted first aid kit round out the options of note. *Michigan State Police Archives*

This collection of Michigan State Police hardware would be worth a fortune today. The aircraft is a Stinson Reliant, and the car is a 1940 Ford Standard with an impressive radio antenna. The motorcycle is a 1937 80 model twin equipped with a radio receiver. *Michigan State Police Archives*

could easily catch cars on this type of road. But as the roads got better and the cars got faster, the bikes lost their value as a police vehicle.

Near wartime in the late thirties, we had fewer bikes out at the posts. Where once we had two bikes, we were reduced to one. Posts were beginning to get busy with complaints. Most every patrol left with a handful of complaints to answer. These took you all over the back roads and on missions that really required the use of a patrol car. I still resent the fact that we had to ride those things in the north, when the nearest pavement was over a hundred miles south. One mile away from the post, and you looked as though someone had dumped a sack of flour on you. We were expected to always look presentable, so we had to pay to clean our own uniforms. The powers that were never fully addressed this problem.

Some of us bought rain suits, similar to coveralls, that were made of rubberized material. We carried them in the saddlebags. If you were going to court or if the roads were dusty, you slipped into the coveralls to try to stay clean. But wearing these suits was frowned upon and, if caught, you were chewed out. It

are safe
WHERE CHILDREN ~~FEAR~~ TO CROSS!

Officer James Pryor and his Harley-Davidson, assist to see kiddies safely across the street near Public School No. 1, Hackensack, N.J.

MAKING crossings safe for children is another of the ADDED MEASURES OF SERVICE in traffic work made possible by Harley-Davidson Police Motorcyles. Seemingly an unimportant routine job—yet how priceless if one child's death is PREVENTED! . . . The new 1937 Harley-Davidsons —with their flexibility, dependability, efficiency, and wide range of economical service — should have an important place in YOUR 1937 Program of Accident Prevention.

A phone call to your nearby Harley-Davidson Dealer NOW will bring a new 1937 model for your inspection. Or write us for literature.

HARLEY-DAVIDSON MOTOR CO., Dept. PU, Milwaukee, Wis.

HARLEY-DAVIDSON
The Police Motorcycle

Harley-Davidson Archives

By the look of the shiny paint on the muffler, I would bet that this is a brand new 1935 Harley. It has the optional speedometer on the tank and "State Police" along with the unit number (fifty-one) lettered on the tank. It is interesting to see a front license plate mounted over the horn. *Maine State Police Archives*

RIGHT
This model 74, 1934 Harley was one of the motorcycles used by the Michigan State Police. On the rear luggage rack is a first-aid kit. The saddlebags are made of leather and are similar to the ones used on a horse. This officer has on a pair of puttees. Also known as "puts" for short, they are leather leggings that fit on top of the shoe and look like high boots. Puttees were common in the early days of police motorcycles. *Michigan State Police Archives*

was the same for head gear. We had to wear the standard police cap, which was built to fly. You could not keep them on unless you wore the chin strap, which then tugged and twisted as the cap tried to blow off. We tried to get them to issue a soft cap like the type issued by the Detroit P.D. At every in-service training school, this was a hot topic. But the answer was always same: without the standard police cap, you didn't look like a trooper. In one training class, with the superintendent present, a trooper was quoted as saying, 'I rode 10,000 miles last summer. And I walked 5,000 after my

A look into the first-aid kit offered in the thirties as an option for Harley police motors. Many departments ordered these kits because their officers were often the first to arrive at the scene of an accident. The officers who carried these kits were the EMT specialists of their day. *Harley-Davidson Archives*

cap!' Thank the lord we have a helmet law now, or they'd still be wearing those stiff hats.

I enjoyed the first couple of years on a bike. After that, it became work. I could not get off until I got promoted. I was in Alpena, then. We only had one bike and didn't use it much. So the day before I left, I took my last ride. It was a nice, sunny, quiet day in August 1940. Sgt. Person let me go for a ride. I went down to Harrisville and East Tawas. When I came back, I put the bike in the garage, and have never been on one since.

Motor Officer Clyde Moore

The front page headline of the Springfield Leader newspaper dated August 1, 1930, read, "Spill Kills Motorbike Officer!" The column heading went on to announce, "Clyde Moore fatally hurt on fire call; Policeman thrown from bike as he paces truck answering alarm; Expires in hospital; Youthful accident victim widely known in Springfield."

According to the reporter, the crash occurred when Moore tried to avoid hitting a Ford touring car parked on the street. The motor officer had just joined up with fire trucks responding to an alarm. A street car had stopped alongside the parked Ford, leav-

ing insufficient room for the motorcycle to squeeze in between. Ofc. Moore was already traveling at a rate of speed too high to stop. To avoid hitting the parked car, he decided to go over the curb.

According to witnesses, he tried to lift up on the handlebars of the motorcycle to get the front wheel over the curb. His efforts had

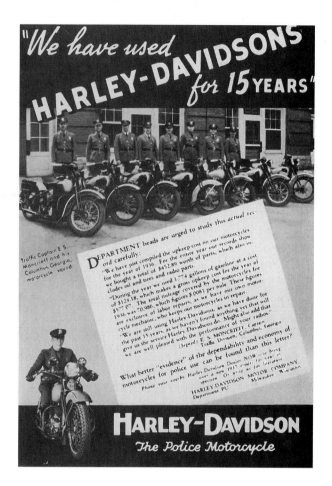

Harley-Davidson Archives

little effect. Instead, as the front wheel hit the curb, Ofc. Moore was thrown over the handlebars, striking his head on a telephone pole. Although breathing at the scene, it is believed he died in the ambulance en route to the hospital. According to the coroner's office, Ofc. Moore suffered a fractured skull, crushed chest, and broken right thigh. Clyde Moore had been with the department less than a year and was twenty-three years of age.

This line-up of motors is from the Oak Park (Illinois) Police Department. While 1936 saw the first Knucklehead motors (61ci), these are 74ci twins. "Oak Park Police" is lettered on the front of the front fender and a very tasteful, small star is painted on the tank.
Harley-Davidson Archives

The Evanston (Illinois) Police Department's motor squad with their 1934 model 74 motors. These officers were the winners of the Grand Prize in a National Traffic Safety Contest. The spotless motors are painted optional police black. The tailpipe on the first motor has a unique flare on the end. *Harley-Davidson Archives*

New Radio Equipped Harley-Davidsons, Dallas, Texas.

The Dallas Police Department's new 1936 motorcycles taken in January 1936. The cold weather necessitated the large bat wings and leg protectors. The color is police silver with black stripes. The front fender plate displays the initials of the Dallas Police Department. *Harley-Davidson Archives*

LEFT
A Harley-Davidson studio shot of a 1938 police model. The front fender mounted light has been replaced by the "Police" placard. The factory offered the optional Harley-Davidson/RCA receive-only radio for $135. The object on the handlebars that looks like a light mounted in reverse is the radio's speaker. The radio's receiver is mounted in the rear carriers in place of saddlebags. The lack of saddlebags meant the officer had no place to store even a pair of gloves—part of the price to be paid for the advance in technology. *Harley-Davidson Archives*

BELOW
In the mid thirties, the color scheme of the California Highway Patrol changed from all-white to black and white. This Knucklehead-powered motor has a tailpipe design unique to the pre-Knucklehead design. Also of note are the officer's straight-leg pants. *California Highway Patrol Archives*

This 1938 61ci Knucklehead retains the front fender light usually deleted for police motorcycles. An "S" shaped tailpipe has been added to the back of the muffler, replacing the exhaust deflector. The rear wheel driven siren is foot actuated with the "L" shaped lever at the rear of the right floorboard. The seat has a unique cover. *California Highway Patrol Archives*

RIGHT
This 1934 model 74 is solid white with a black frame and accessories. The unit number is painted on the toolbox and the word "Police" is lettered on the tank in place of the Harley-Davidson logo. *Salt Lake City, Utah, Police Archives*

CHAPTER 3

Radios: Call boxes to Multi-Channels

The early motor officer went about his job alone. At the beginning of his shift, he met with fellow officers and supervisors, then left to patrol his beat. Early motor officers were essentially cowboys riding the range. If a motor officer on patrol wanted to be included in an event, it was not uncommon for him to follow a passing patrol car to its destination.

The police call box, which began to appear as early as 1905, enabled the motor officer to communicate to headquarters from the field. At regularly scheduled times, he would call in to check for messages and to be given assignments. These assignments could entail going to another part of town or could require replacing an officer out of service in another area. The call boxes did not provide an immediate response. The time lag between receiving a call at the station and assigning a motor officer to an assignment was lengthy. Any crime in progress was probably long over by the time an officer got the call.

In the late 1920s, radios were beginning to appear in squad cars. They were cumbersome, tube-type units, limited to receiving messages only. In 1931, a few units were installed on police motorcycles. These early radios, designed by Harley-Davidson, were expensive and unreliable. Their unreliability was due in part to the rough road conditions to which they were subjected daily. It was bad enough that the radio was attached to the back of a machine that vibrated at its own frequency. Add to that an unsprung rear wheel above which the radio was mounted, and short electronic life resulted.

Harley-Davidson first offered radios as a police option in 1935. The radio receiver was priced at $75 and the buyer could specify the

The Wichita Police Department had the first radio receiver west of the Mississippi. It was installed on this 1931 74 model. The receiver is mounted on the rear luggage rack. The speaker is the elongated, curved funnel-shaped object originating below the tank. This design never did see widespread use. *Wichita, Kansas, Police Archives*

"wavelength," or frequency. This radio was mounted on the rear luggage rack. In 1938, the price of a radio receiver had increased to $135 and the unit was manufactured by RCA. In the late thirties, there were two distinct antennae for motorcycle use: the traditional whip antenna and a screen type. Both were mounted on the rear of the bike.

Two-way radios first appeared in the mid- to late-forties. The Neenah and Menasha (Wisconsin) police departments were the first to use them. This radio was jointly developed by Harley-Davidson and RCA. The first installations were on Servi-Cars, probably due to the large rear trunk space available for the hardware. The first two-way radios for solo police use appeared in 1948 in the form of a twenty-seven-pound unit described by Harley as "compact." It was attached to the rear

In October 1938, CHP Sergeant Les Williams inspects the first CHP installation of a motorcycle radio receiver. It was tuned to 2414 kilocycles to receive the Ventura, California, police broadcasts. The speaker is mounted on the handlebars behind the large twin lights. *California Highway Patrol Archives*

carrier frame, taking the space formerly occupied by the saddlebags. On the left was the receiver and on the right, the transmitter. It had an eighteen-inch whip antenna mounted on the receiver box. It operated on the 152 megacycle band, or VHF Hi-band. A speaker box with volume and

RIGHT
October 1937 advertisement introduces the 1938 police models. It features the Harley/RCA manufactured radio receiver and its screen-type antenna. A big complaint of these early radio installations was the lack of storage space. *Harley-Davidson Archives*

BELOW
These three 1934 model 74 motors belong to the Lake County (Illinois) Sheriff's Department. The large box on the rear carrier is the radio. These tube type receivers took a lot of abuse over the unsprung rear wheel. The siren and a "Sheriff" placard were mounted on the front fender. To each side of the headlight are small accessory lights, not a usual police accessory. *Harley-Davidson Archives*

GET SET FOR GREATER TRAFFIC SAFETY

WITH NEW—1938 HARLEY-DAVIDSON POLICE MOTORCYCLES

★ Prepare now to cut down the 1938 traffic toll through efficient patrol of streets and highways. Many cities have established enviable records proving the outstanding value of having uniformed officers on motorcycles where they can be seen — where their presence puts the "brakes" on recklessness and speeding.

Equip your squads with the new 1938 Harley-Davidson Police Motorcycles. New features include, magnetic handlebar-operated speedometer hand stop, red and green signal lights for oil pressure and generator charge, streamlined siren, greatly strengthened frames, inter-connected brake shoes in service brakes, timing gears run in oil bath, and compression-type oil pipe connections. These and other improvements and refinements make these new 1938 models the ideal vehicles for fast, dependable, low-cost police service.

Phone your nearby Harley-Davidson Dealer NOW—to bring over a new 1938 model for your inspection. Or write us for literature.

HARLEY-DAVIDSON MOTOR CO. *Dept.* PU, Milwaukee, Wis.

HARLEY-DAVIDSON
The Police Motorcycle

New high impedance screen type antenna, up away from dirt, grime, and grease. Compact and light in weight. Saddle bag mounting of radio receiver brings weight way down low.

squelch controls was mounted on top of the handlebars. A press-to-talk microphone was used, similar in size and shape to what is used today.

These early radios were large, heavy, and unreliable. They consumed all available storage

This Michigan State Police trooper, wearing a great pair of gauntlet gloves, looks relaxed on his 1937 model 80 as he parks at one of Michigan's Great Lake beach parks. The rear racks hold a receive-only radio. Above the taillight is a screen type antenna. *Michigan State Police Archives*

BELOW AND NEXT PAGE
Two excellent views of the same 1950 FL. It's equipped with the standard Police Group (of accessories) which includes: front safety guards in black, jiffy stand, 5.00x16 wheels and tires, air-cleaner, rear wheel siren, speedometer, hand control, and deluxe saddle. Radio equipment is the Motorola Uni-Channel Sensicon two-way dispatch model with a maximum power output of 12 watts. Because these radios were tube-type, they required over thirty seconds to warm up. Suppressors were installed on the spark plugs to reduce radio interference. Although most departments were using windshields by the late forties, this factory model has not been fitted with one. *Harley-Davidson Archives*

space. The transmission power was between seven and ten watts and drained the limited six-volt power supply. To ensure sufficient power to transmit, the officer had to keep the engine running at a high speed. The noise of the engine tended to drown out the voice of the officer, making reception inaudible. The power drain in the receive mode was a sizable 9.5 amps. Because of the high current drain, it was recommended that the radio be turned off prior to starting the engine. Damage to the transmitter's power supply could also result from starting the engine with the radio on. Once turned on, it took thirty seconds for the tubes to warm sufficiently for operation.

The 1949 order form listed several radio options for police use. General Electric, Motorola, and RCA all offered radios. The least expensive was the receive-only model, an option at $225. Motorola manufactured the two-way radios and sold them for a whopping $530 (the big twin motorcycle alone listed for $750). A 1949 FL with full police equipment could list for as much as

$1,500. The electrical systems were redesigned to take the additional load. Special generators, regulators, and radio interference suppressors were optionally installed. This option was called the Radio Application Kit and included a 44amp battery. The cost of this kit for a solo was $92, and $43 for the Servi-Car.

Between 1949 and 1957, police radios changed little. Harley offered a model by Link Vetric along with Motorola's model. In June 1957, Motorola introduced the "Dispatcher Radiophone," representing a significant design change. No longer an adaptation of an automobile unit, this radio was designed specifically for motorcycles. It was a smaller package featuring the adaptation of transistors. These low-power devices replaced the high drain of the previous tube-type radios. Power consumption was now down to one amp to receive and fifteen amps to transmit. Low-band output took up to twelve watts and high band used from seven to eight, a significant improvement. This compact unit was

LAX ENFORCEMENT *Breeds* CARELESSNESS

RADIO Equipment

New high impedance siren type antenna, as away from dirt, grime and grease. Compact and light in weight. Improves telephone. Saddle bag mounting of radio telescope brings weight low down low and makes for easier handling of motorcycle.

and CARELESSNESS BREEDS ACCIDENTS

Get at the root of accidents by wiping out carelessness. Let both pedestrians and motorists know they MUST "watch their step."

It is a well established fact that uniformed officers on motorcycles — patrolling streets and highways 24 hours a day — put an effective brake on carelessness. This method keeps officers where they can be seen — where their presence is felt — where it has an instant and telling effect on behavior. . . . To curb the careless, the reckless, and the wanton violators — to make enforcement something to be respected — yes, even feared — mount your squads on 1937 Harley-Davidson Police Motorcycles. The new models have many improved features to make them more than ever the ideal vehicle for fast, dependable, low-cost police service.

Phone your nearby Harley-Davidson Dealer NOW — to bring over a new 1937 model for your inspection. Or write us for literature.

HARLEY-DAVIDSON MOTOR COMPANY
Department PU,   Milwaukee, Wisconsin

HARLEY-DAVIDSON
The Police Motorcycle

OPPOSITE PAGE TOP LEFT
Advertisement from February 1937. *Harley-Davidson Archives*

OPPOSITE PAGE TOP RIGHT AND BOTTOM
Although not as popular as the solo, the sidecar models were used in the past and are still in use today. This is a 1951 FLS (the "S" denotes sidecar gearing). Of special note on this model is the Link-Vetric Radio. Although it was offered as a police option, this radio is rarely seen. Note the metal first-aid kit on top of the rear fender. *Harley-Davidson Archives*

RIGHT
The radio that revolutionized mobile communications. The Motorola Transistor Dispatcher, first introduced in 1957, was a self-contained, fork-mounted installation for solos. With the introduction of the Duo-Glide in 1958, radios could be safely mounted over the rear tire. The basic chassis was half the size and weight of previous radios. This installation uses a snap-on, vinyl cover. *Harley-Davidson Archives*

A Motorola Dispatcher speaker and microphone are mounted on the handlebars. Volume and squelch controls are on the top of the speaker box. The microphone is standard, press-to-talk technology. *Harley-Davidson Archives*

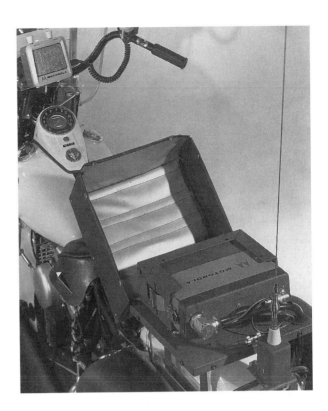

designed to mount on the handlebars of a solo motorcycle to avoid the shock of the unsprung rear wheel. Radio units for Servi-Cars were mounted in the trunk, with the speaker control unit on the handlebars. The speaker and microphone were now weatherproofed. Speaker volume increased by about fifty percent, providing audible reception at speed. The cost for this new Motorola unit was $635.

With the introduction in 1958 of the rear sprung Duo-Glide, the new radio could be mounted again on the back of the motorcycle. These smaller units mounted on top of the fender, with speaker and microphone up front. Officers often increased the volume control as they drove along the road to compensate for the noise. As they came to a stop, they often forgot to reduce the volume. As soon as the dispatcher began to broadcast a message, the officer scrambled to reduce the now blaring volume. A common prank motor officers played on one another was to turn up the volume on a radio unit while the officer was away from his motor. Upon his return, the unsuspecting officer would start his motor and be nearly blown off with the first broadcast!

In 1966, Harley stopped offering optional radios. This move coincided with the adoption

of a standard twelve-volt electrical system. No doubt the complexity of matching six- and twelve-volt systems and radios was more trouble than it was worth. Fortunately, Motorola offered a six- to twelve-volt conversion kit. As more vendors developed lighter, multi-functional radios,

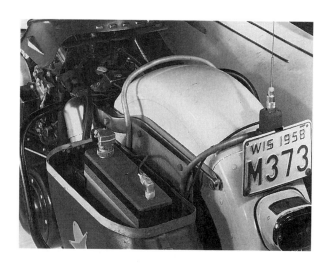

The introduction of the Duo-Glide allowed the radios to be installed in the saddlebags. The small black box in front of the safety guard is the voltage regulator, standard on all 1958 police models. *Harley-Davidson Archives*

On what appears to be a winter's day in Richmond, Virginia, a motor officer opens the rear compartment of his Servi-Car, giving him access to a two-way radio. The cross bracing on the underside of the lid gave the lid the strength to support someone sitting on top. *Richmond, Virginia, Police Dept. Archives*

OPPOSITE PAGE BOTTOM
A 1958 Servi-Car with the new Motorola two-way radio. This was the latest compact design that utilized transistors, revolutionizing two-way police communications. This model is also equipped with the easy-opening rear handle. *Harley-Davidson Archives*

BELOW
In 1960, when the rotating beacon was ordered, the left-side pursuit light was deleted. Mounted on the front forks are small, directional signals. The radio was mounted in a weatherproof box over the rear wheel. *Tampa, Florida, Police Archives*

Motorola radio installation on a 1961 Duo-Glide. The weatherproof cover was made out of plastic. *Harley-Davidson Archives*

RIGHT
A motor officer's view of a radio speaker and microphone. Note the lettering on the speedometer of this 1965 FL, indicating "Police Special." *Harley-Davidson Archives*

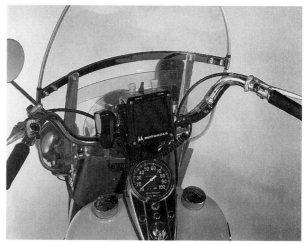

The size of the radio box has not changed much since the late fifties, but the contents have. Today's radios are lighter and more powerful with the ability to transmit and receive on several frequencies. The reliability of today's radios is equal to that of the AM/FM radio installed in your car.

Today's radio has multi-channel capability with scan. The small circular object to the left of the radio is the jack receptacle for the officer's helmet cord.

CHAPTER 4

The Servi-Car: Mark that Tire!

The Servi-Car first appeared in late 1931, available for sale with the 1932 models. Conceived and designed in the late twenties, the concept was simple. Design a motorcycle that anyone can ride, with available space for storage. There were package trucks based on the sidecar design, but they required the skill of an experienced rider. With the even balance of the tricycle design, almost anyone could ride a Servi-Car.

Servi-Cars were initially designed for automobile service departments. In the thirties, it was not unusual for a car salesman to bring a new model car out to a prospective customer's house for a firsthand look or test drive. Repair service was handled at the home, too. The dealer's mechanic drove to the owner's home on a Servi-Car. Simple repairs could be done with tools carried in the Servi-Car's spacious rear body box. If the vehicle needed to be taken to the dealership for more serious work, the mechanic could drive the car, with the Servi-Car in tow. Model GA was equipped with a front tow bar that could be easily attached to the car's rear bumper. When finished, the mechanic drove back to the customer's house, unhooked the tow bar, and motored back to the dealership on the Servi-Car. The large box offered another benefit to the business owner—it provided a convenient surface for advertisement.

One very happy looking officer patrols the streets of Orlando in 1948 on his Servi-Car. The clipboard on the handlebars holds the daily hot-sheet listing stolen cars. *Orlando, Florida, Police Archives*

Law enforcement agencies quickly adopted the Servi-Car for their use. It provided them with an all-weather utility vehicle. Officers new to the traffic unit were assigned to them in hopes of eventually moving up to "real motors." Most solo riders looked down their noses at the tricycle as a motorcycle designed for those unable to balance. Its longevity proved its true worth.

Most Servi-Cars were used for parking enforcement. Harley even offered a tire marking

The Tampa Police Department had this fully optioned 1961 Servi-Car in service. This Servi-Car was a parking patrol vehicle, as evidenced by the tire marking stick on the rear compartment lid and the shifter located on the right side. Right-hand shift models offered a left-hand throttle for ease in tire marking. Notice the small accessory parking lights on the front fork and the additional rear facing lights on the side of the box just above the fender-mounted light. This unit was not painted in the traditional police silver or black. It appears to be in one of the optional colors for 1961 of either Pepper Red or Skyline Blue with white trim. *Tampa, Florida, Police Dept. Archives*

stick as an option. Tire marking has not changed over the decades: The officer rode along the line of cars parked along a curb and marked a tire on each car with a white marker. Servi-Cars were even offered with right-hand shift and left-hand throttle. This allowed the parking enforcement officer to drive along a line of parked cars, marking tires with his right hand while still modulating speed with the left hand. At the limit of the posted parking, the officer returned, riding past the line of previously marked cars. Those still present with a mark on the tire received a citation.

The Servi-Car's three wheels gave the officer a steady platform to easily park and dismount. Servi-Cars were equipped with a hand shifted, three-speed transmission, and a reverse gear. The reverse gear gave the officer great flexibility in parking and maneuvering. In the December 1943 issue of *The Enthusiast*, Joseph Peters wrote about the wartime use of Servi-Cars at the Badger Ordinance Works: "For the parking lot details, a Harley-Davidson Servi-Car is used

Reduce TRAFFIC CONGESTION with SERVI-CARS !

Cars parked overlong only add to traffic congestion. Eliminate this particular problem through a faster and more thorough check-up with Harley-Davidson Servi-Cars. Enables officers to cover many times the area possible by any other method.

The Servi-Car method helps you cut down traffic congestion — keeps parking hogs on the move — gives "regular" motorists a chance — gives retail merchants a "break."

What's more, Servi-Cars will release officers sorely needed for other duties — will make more men available to apprehend speeders, reckless drivers and other law-breakers who are a menace to your community.

Yes, Servi-Cars and Harley-Davidson Motorcycles make a wonderful combination for efficient traffic control. . . . . *See your Harley-Davidson Dealer now — or write us.*
HARLEY-DAVIDSON MOTOR COMPANY
DEPARTMENT PU   MILWAUKEE, WIS.

HARLEY-DAVIDSON
The Police Motorcycle

The Beaumont, Texas, police are Harley-Davidson equipped... Servi-Cars supplementing the city's efficient motorcycle squad.

May 1937 advertisement for a police Servi-Car.
Harley-Davidson Archives

and too much cannot be said for this three-wheeled vehicle. Its ability to turn short, carry extra passengers, and its easy riding qualities have completely justified its purchase."

The large rear box was perfect for the accident investigation officer. It held his equipment and first-aid kit. The forward tilting box lid could be upholstered for the comfort of the occasional passenger. Optional handles for the sides of the box were available, giving the rear passenger something to hold onto. This rear box could double as an ice chest or cooler for police social events. One police department even modified the rear box to carry a police dog, making the Servi-Car a little K-9 unit.

Another police use for Servi-Cars was parade duty and funeral escorts. Both of these assignments were low-speed adventures. While stable at low speeds, the Servi-Car did not offer the rider the same degree of acceleration and maneuverability as a solo motor.

The Servi-Car was designed like a trike and it handled like a trike. When riding a Servi-Car, officers regularly assigned to solo motors were an interesting sight to see. They usually drove them too fast, forgetting they were on a three-wheeler. Rounding corners was a spectacle. Expecting the vehicle to behave like a two-wheeler, the rider would lean his body into the turn, but the Servi-Car doesn't lean. The officer looked as if he would lean right off the vehicle! One officer who rode them said the most fun was in the winter. He'd find a snow covered parking lot and spin donuts on the slippery surface.

The Servi-Car design was simple but elegant. While there were other three-wheeled designs available, none were as well thought out and executed. The design was not a quick adaptation of a pair of rear wheels to the existing machine, but an entirely new design. The rear frame was a rather complex design utilizing a combination of leaf and coil springs. The rear axle was an adaptation of an automotive design with a chain-drive sprocket driving both rear wheels. The Servi-Car's overall length was 100 inches and the rear tread was 42 inches. This wide tread enabled the rider to drive in auto tire paths in snowy weather. The rear axle housing of early models contained the rear brake, adapted from a solo. Later models had the brakes on the rear wheel hubs. The engine for all Servi-Cars was the DS-45. This 21hp engine, first introduced in 1929, served faithfully until 1974.

Technical changes over the life of the Servi-Car were few. Hydra-Glide forks first appeared on solo motors in 1949. They were offered as an option for the Servi-Car in 1952, at a cost of $10.25. They remained an option until 1958 when they became standard equipment. Other significant changes over the life of the design included electric starters (1964) and fiberglass box and rear fenders (1966). Police agencies used the model GA without the tow bar. The electric start models were given the model designator, GE.

Police equipment from the factory was plentiful. Over the life of the machine, Harley offered three different styles of front wheel sirens, all either hand or foot controlled. Rear wheel sirens were available but rarely seen. Pursuit lights were of the same configuration as those on the solo bikes for each model year. The earliest implementation of two-way radios was on the Servi-Car in 1948. The Servi-Car offered the space and shock-mounted isolation of the rear box for installation.

Today, the Servi-Car has been replaced by many efficient, but much less interesting

The Police Department of Colorado Springs operated this right-hand shift 1960 Servi-Car. Note the upholstered box lid and handles for the occasional passenger. The radio is installed in the box. The knobs for volume and squelch are on the lower edge of the speaker plate. *Colorado Springs, Colorado, Police Dept. Archives*

LEFT
Omaha Police Department's parking enforcement officers drove this 1961 model. The tire marking stick is securely mounted on the rear of the box lid. Added to the rear wheels are stylish trim rings. *Omaha, Nebraska, Police Dept. Archives*

pieces of equipment. The few remaining Servi-Cars have been entombed in police museums across the nation. They were durable contributors to police work for decades. Today, they only provide us with fond memories.

ABOVE
This restored 1947 GA model Servi-Car has a non-standard black-and-white paint scheme. Merchants used the rear of the box for advertising. This police department uses the space to clearly mark it as a police vehicle.

Parking enforcement was the meat and potatoes of Servi-Car duty.

ABOVE
The light bar with twin red lights was the same as the one offered for solo motors in 1947. The rear spoke wheels were subsequently replaced with disk type automotive wheels.

TOP LEFT
This is without a doubt the most attractive of the three front-wheel-mounted sirens available for Servi-Cars. It was cable-actuated by hand or foot lever. When actuated, it pivoted to allow the knurled drive to come in contact with the tire. This spun the siren to achieve the desired sound level. Notice the beautifully styled front fender light. This light could be deleted in favor of an optional plate with the word "Police" on it.

BOTTOM LEFT
The left-hand shifter operated a transmission with three forward gears and one reverse gear. Reverse was necessary to maneuver the Servi-Car more easily.

ABOVE
This is a mid-sixties mix of Servi-Cars from Richmond. Of special note is that they are all right-hand shift models, and they all have electric front fender sirens. *Richmond, Virginia, Police Dept. Archives*

BELOW
A late-sixties line-up of Richmond's Servi-Car unit. These models have the fiberglass box and very large bat wings and leg protectors. By the absence of leaves on the trees, it looks like late fall or winter when more protection against cold weather is necessary. *Richmond, Virginia, Police Dept. Archives*

A 1969 assemblage of Richmond's patrol vehicles: two Ford products with four wheels each, a 1hp four-legged model, and a new Servi-Car. *Richmond, Virginia, Police Dept. Archives*

LEFT TOP
A Richmond traffic officer motions traffic
around a stalled automobile. The back of his
1968 Servi-Car is clearly marked as a police
vehicle. *Richmond, Virginia, Police Dept. Archives*

LEFT BOTTOM
A late-sixties mix of Servi-Cars in Richmond.
Both fiberglass and metal box versions are
shown. *Richmond, Virginia, Police Dept. Archives*

ABOVE
The color of this 1950 Servi-Car appears to be
silver, optional for police only. Notice the radio
antenna on the box lid. *Harley-Davidson Archives*

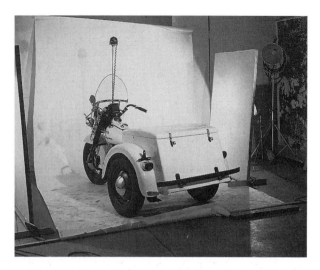

RIGHT TOP
This profile of a 1958 Servi-Car shows the subtle but stylish swoop of the rear fender and rear compartment. Styling details like these are among the reasons Harleys have had a tremendous appeal over the years. *Harley-Davidson Archives*

RIGHT BOTTOM
A 1960 photo illustration of a silver Servi-Car with a handlebar mounted two-way radio. *Harley-Davidson Archives*

A 1963 Servi-Car is in the studio to have its portrait taken. This model has the Motorola radio speaker on top of the handlebars. Notice the optional pursuit light at the full extension of its telescoping mount. *Harley-Davidson Archives*

BELOW
1958 Servi-Car with a handlebar mounted Motorola two-way radio. There are two hand levers on the left handlebar grip. The larger of the two is for the front brake and the smaller lever controls the front-mounted siren. *Harley-Davidson Archives*

ABOVE
This early-fifties scene was repeated thousands of times across the country. The motorist's time has expired, and the officer is doing his duty by writing a parking citation. This unit has a Motorola two-way radio mounted in the rear box. This Servi-Car is unique with its twin front lights and rear wheel driven siren (just visible near the front lower corner of the rear fender). Judging by the officer's jacket, large fairing, and leg protectors on the Servi-Car, it must be winter. Also of note is the sheepskin cover on the seat. *Harley-Davidson Archives*

LEFT
A 1960 Servi-Car viewed from above clearly shows the strengthening ribs stamped into the box lid. The two latches are on the rear edge. Additional rear facing lights are above the standard stop lights. The radio speaker, with its volume and squelch control knobs on top, is mounted on the handlebars. Near the right-hand grip is the microphone. *Harley-Davidson Archives*

This 1961 Servi-Car is about to have its clutch adjusted. The small cover has been removed, exposing the clutch adjusting screw and lock nut. To the upper left is the circular chain inspection opening. The left-side tank is the fuel tank. On its lower rear edge is the fuel cutoff valve. *Harley-Davidson Archives*

ABOVE
Photo illustration of a 1955 Servi-Car. The tank emblem was carried over to the 1956 model year. *Harley-Davidson Archives*

LEFT TOP
A 1953 Servi-Car in police silver with the "Police" fender plate, optional for an additional $3.90. *Harley-Davidson Archives*

LEFT BOTTOM
No need to get off your Servi-Car when you have the optional tire marking stick. *Harley-Davidson Archives*

Right-hand side of a 1958 Servi-Car with its flathead 45ci engine. The pedal is for the rear brakes. To the left is the kick starter. Above the engine is the oil tank. *Harley-Davidson Archives*

Six brand spanking new 1936 Servi-Cars. These Denver, Colorado, police units were equipped with receive-only radios. *Harley-Davidson Archives*

One officer and Servi-Car at Austin, Texas now do the car marking work formerly done by four officers on foot.

1936 photo with the original caption from the Harley archives. *Harley-Davidson Archives*

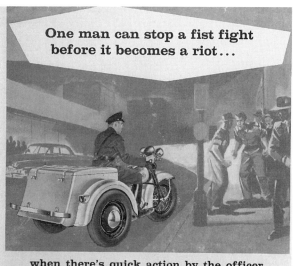

One man can stop a fist fight
before it becomes a riot...

when there's quick action by the officer
on a radio-equipped Harley-Davidson Servi-Car

ON the scene in seconds, this Servi-Car mounted officer puts a fast
damper on heated tempers. No chance for it to grow into a riot,
require calling for reinforcements.

It's but one of many reasons most communities noted for excellent
enforcement are putting more and more of their officers on Harley-
Davidson police motorcycles.

Fast, mobile and radio-dispatched Servi-Cars help you get more effective use of your current manpower . . . make your force more mobile
without going overboard on equipment and its maintenance and service.

Cost data on Harley-Davidson police motorcycle operation, maintenance and depreciation show it amounts to only a fraction of that for
other vehicles. Why not get the complete story from your dealer or write
direct for comprehensive literature. HARLEY-DAVIDSON MOTOR
COMPANY, Milwaukee 1, Wisconsin.

Free booklet is yours
for the asking . . .

This 16-page book, "More Effective
Round the Clock Police Power with
Harley-Davidson Motorcycles", in-
cludes assignment data as well as
specifications on both three-wheel
Servi-Car and two-wheel Solo Models.

HARLEY-DAVIDSON police motorcycles

1957 advertisement for a police Servi-Car. *Harley-Davidson Archives*

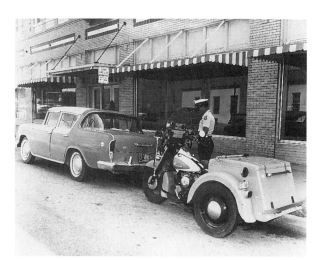

**Two vehicles from the past that are gone but
not forgotten: a Nash Rambler and a Servi-Car.
The Servi-Car is a 1961 model. It is fully
optioned with Motorola "Dispatcher" radio,
rotating emergency light, Hydra-Glide
windshield, and adjustable tire marking stick.**
Tampa, Florida, Police Dept. Archives

Four Servi-Car officers and their mounts outside of the Tampa motor pool garage. All of these Harleys are right-hand shift, left-hand throttle models. *Tampa, Florida, Police Dept. Archives*

CHAPTER 5

The Forties: War Era Machines

In 1940, over 3,500 law enforcement agencies were using Harley-Davidson motorcycles. The police business was an important part of the company's overall market. During the next three decades, motor officers benefited from innovations that made their machines more comfortable, more stable, and quicker to start. Of course, we're talking about the Hydra-Glide, Duo-Glide, and Electra-Glide.

In 1941, the new line of motorcycles included a 74ci version of the EL with two improvements: a more efficient oil pump and a better clutch. It wouldn't be until after the war, in 1947, that the 1941 model would be updated again. With each new improvement in the motorcycle came more comfort, safety, or performance for the motor officer. With the introduction in 1949 of the Hydra-Glide Fork, the motor officer had a more stable and improved ride. Rubber-mounted handlebars helped reduce vibration. This was also the first year of the full-skirted air-flow fender design.

During World War II, Harley-Davidson's production level for the civilian market was cut back, due to the shortage of supplies and the need to fulfill military and police requirements. Law enforcement agencies were being called upon now to patrol and protect locations considered vital to the national defense. The demand for police motorcycles by police departments sustained dealers who, because of the war, could not obtain enough bikes to meet the demands of their civilian customers.

Harley-Davidson was permitted to sell new motorcycles to police agencies, but not without much paperwork. In 1943, for example, the Federal government allowed 137 police departments to purchase new motorcycles from

During the years of World War II, the California Highway Patrol escorted military convoys along the coast highways. The officers assigned were given special equipment to cope with the possibility of a sneak attack from the Pacific Ocean. The backpack contains a gas mask and on the outside is a metal helmet. Their standard revolver was augmented with the Thompson .45 caliber submachine gun. *California Highway Patrol Archives*

Harley-Davidson, but only after a process of substantial documentation. Municipalities completed their paperwork indicating their need and intended use. Harley-Davidson then filed this paperwork with the War Production Board for final approval.

During the war years, Harley-Davidson could not use nickel alloy for cylinders—and police motors were wearing out the silicon alloy substitute after about 600 to 800 miles because of idling to keep their batteries charged to allow radio use. In response, chrome was used instead, increasing longevity to 20,000 miles. Around 1947, Harley-Davidson was finally able to resume full production of its civilian motorcycle line. The enormous demand for civilian motorcycles by re-

I'm sure this California Highway Patrol officer lost the bet and had to lay down his motor for the photo. I don't know if I would want to be behind a leaking gas tank, with someone shooting at me, while I'm blazing away with a machine gun. *California Highway Patrol Archives*

turning servicemen who had ridden Harleys during wartime resulted in a postwar boom for the company.

In 1942, speed limits were reduced in an effort to conserve gasoline. In addition, all production of civilian automobiles and light trucks was halted by federal order. In 1942 and 1943, production of Harley-Davidson motorcycles peaked at a little over 29,000 units each year, designated primarily for military and police use. Many law enforcement agencies now had additional paramilitary duties for which they were responsible. The California Highway Patrol hired an additional 300 officers during this time. Their expanded duties now included escorting munitions

shipments and patrolling the coastline along the beach. The CHP also worked with the FBI and the military to prevent sabotage and to protect the highway system and manufacturing plants. To carry out these activities, motor officers were equipped with Thompson submachine guns, and carried gas masks and military helmets in backpacks.

Cincinnati Police Department

In 1940, the Police Chief of the Cincinnati Police Department established a Police Safety School to teach police personnel the proper way to operate a motor vehicle. It was found that at least fifteen percent of the police officers had never even driven an automobile. It's conceivable that the motor officers were similarly lacking in training or experience on motorcycles. On April 27, 1940, Patrolman Robert Leigh, a ten-year veteran of the department, was killed when an automobile pulled out from a private drive-

A common activity of motorcycle duty is parade and VIP escort. General Jimmy Doolittle was being honored in St. Louis. His car was flanked by Harleys. *St. Louis, Missouri, Police Archives*

across from police headquarters. During the forties, the number of solo motorcycles used by the Cincinnati Police Department dropped each year, while the number of Servi-Cars increased.

By 1944, motorcycle patrolmen working for the Cincinnati Police department received an extra $126.36 annually in hazardous duty pay. As of November 1, 1944, solo motorcycles were no longer used in the apprehension of moving traffic violators. Instead, they concentrated on auto accident investigation and parking violations. No expla-

BELOW
Two California Highway Patrol sergeants in their black-and-white Harley sidecar. The light configuration with two large headlights is unusual. The officers' uniforms are interesting, with one officer wearing a bow tie and the other wearing a standard necktie. One officer's leather jacket has a fur collar and the other has a plain collar. *California Highway Patrol Archives*

way and into his path of travel. Officer Leigh's likeness, astride his Harley-Davidson motorcycle, is etched on the Cincinnati Police Memorial

Are these motor officers smiling because they get to ride Harley's or because they get to escort Miss Bonnie Lou Barker, Queen of the 1949 Toy Bowl football game? That was the first year for Hydra-Glide front forks and the only year they were half bright and half black. Hydra-Glide forks were the biggest improvement in ride and handling to date. This motorcycle is painted in police silver and has a foot-operated siren, but no radio. *Mobile, Alabama, Police Dept. Archives*

nation is offered as to why "pursuits" were discontinued in this department. Maybe for the same reasons they are discouraged today (Department liability, cost of litigation and settlement, and insurance rates all increase with every accident-related, high-speed pursuit). By 1949, all motorcycles in Cincinnati were equipped with one-way radios, as were all other motor vehicles in the fleet. And by the end of 1949, all sidecar rigs had been discontinued.

Lansing Police Department

In 1942, the city of Lansing, Michigan, created an Accident Investigation Bureau in hopes of reducing the number of deaths and injuries resulting from traffic accidents. Officers took courses at Northwestern University Traffic Institute to enable them to effectively investigate, report, and keep records of traffic accidents. With this information, enforcement and education were applied accordingly in hopes of reducing future accidents in these high-accident locations. Motor officers were assigned to ride their newly purchased Harley-Davidsons on patrol in these areas, assisting investigators as needed.

V-Twin Tales: Harleys on Patrol

Captain Roy Phillips

Retired Captain Roy Phillips of the Charlotte-Mecklenburg (North Carolina) Police Department recalled his experiences rid-

This photo of six Harleys was taken at the Alabama State Docks, Port of Mobile, in November 1942. The two motorcycles on the left are 1941 or 1942 models. The four on the right are 1940 models. Notice the difference in windshield and bat wing design. Rudy Reeves, the officer on the left, was killed two weeks after this photo was taken when he struck an open manhole. *Mobile, Alabama, Police Dept. Archives*

ing Harley-Davidson motorcycles on patrol:

"My first contact with the Charlotte Police Department's motorcycle squad was in 1935. I was ten years old and in the fourth grade. Two of Charlotte's motorcycle officers worked the school crossings, helping kids safely cross the streets. One day as Officer Ramsey was helping me cross the street, he asked me what I wanted to be when I grew up. I told him I wanted to be a motorcycle officer.

"I joined the Charlotte Police Department in 1947, and in 1948, was transferred from the Patrol Bureau to the traffic division and assigned to the motorcycle squad.

"The department furnished a police escort for all funeral processions. A motorcycle was often assigned to escort the procession as far as the cemetery entrance, at which point the officer would leave. On one particular morning as I was providing the usual escort, I noticed an American flag draped over the coffin. Upon reaching the cemetery entrance, I got off my motorcycle, stood at attention, took my cap off, and placed it over my heart. So began my own personal tradition of always paying my respects to those I escorted to the cemetery.

"One morning at roll call, Captain Henkle jumped on the motorcycle officers to put more miles on their motorcycles. We tried to tell him that working school crossings, escorting funerals, sitting up on hazardous intersections, going to court, and investigating traffic accidents was cutting down on our mileage. The captain said he wasn't buying our excuses and demanded we put more miles on the motorcycles. Several hours later, I ran across Officer "Sleepy" Norton in Latta Park, lying in the shade of a tree. Sleepy's motorcycle was jacked up on the jiffy stand with the motorcycle running in second gear. I asked Sleepy what in the world was going on. He told me he was seeing to it that the Captain got more miles on his motorcycles. With the motorcycle being air cooled, it sure wasn't doing the motorcycle any good running in second gear in 90 degree heat!

"One fall day, I was siting in some woods on my motorcycle on Freedom Drive, when a car came by at 80mph. I gave chase and pulled up beside the speeder who had stopped for a red light. When I advised the speeder that I was going to write him a citation for speeding, he sniped, 'I hope you got your quota for the day.' I advised him, as I did everyone who gave me that line, 'Oh, I don't have a quota. Chief Littlejohn lets me write as many tickets as I want to!' Then I said I'd rather write him a ticket than escort him to a cemetery."

Motor Officer Roderick G. Welsh

Roderick G. Welsh rode motors for the Long Beach (California) Police Department during the forties. His written journal of personal war

The St. Louis Motor unit in the early forties. Can you imagine the sound of all of these Harleys riding by? *St. Louis, Missouri, Police Dept. Archives*

Sgt. Ruff of the St. Louis Police Department is doing his job by writing tickets. His motor is a 1941–1946 Harley. It is radio equipped and is unique with a right-hand shifter. *St. Louis, Missouri, Police Dept. Archives*

stories includes this one, "Hayride with Rod on his Iron Horse."

"In Long Beach, California, there are two main streets, both six lanes wide. Pacific Coast Highway runs north and south, and Long Beach Boulevard runs east and west. On Long Beach Boulevard there was a stretch of road with about three miles between signals—a temptation to exceed the 35mph speed limit.

"As was my habit, I parked off the highway at the halfway point. On this day, I heard a vehicle coming at a high rate of speed. I cranked my motor on, and when he passed, I gave chase. When I attained his speed, I punched the button on my handlebars, freezing the speedometer reading, I later found out, at 62mph. Then, I

started to catch up with him.

"He was approximately one-quarter mile from Pacific Coast Highway when the signal changed. He made it through, but I couldn't. When I hit my brakes, they broke. I was helpless to stop with six lanes crossing in front of me. Passing directly in front was a hay truck and trailer. I had to make a split-second decision. Do I lay it down and try to slide under him, or if possible, go behind?

"I wouldn't be writing this if I hadn't slipped between the other two lanes. It was my luck that the Lord was with me and I coast-

These five Harleys represent the war year model, identical between 1941 and 1946. They are all receiver-only equipped. Facing the rider on the right side of the handlebars is the radio speaker, resembling a rear-facing light. Two items of interest are the saddlebags hung on the radio racks and the right-hand shifters. *St. Louis, Missouri, Police Dept. Archives*

Changing shifts: Motor officers leave the department garage in the early forties. *St. Louis, Missouri, Police Dept. Archives*

ed a block and got off my horse. When I looked at my kneecaps, they were bouncing like popcorn popping!"

Roderick G. Welsh shares another of his stories from his years riding Harleys with the Long Beach Police Department. This one is called, "Flying with Rod, the Lucky."

"If you are old enough to remember a man named Henry Kaiser, you will remember that he was building 'Liberty Ships'—almost one a day—at the CALSHIP Shipyard in Long Beach.

"It was our job to put cones on the eight-lane road leading into the shipyard, while observing traffic going in and out. I had put my cones out and was riding back on my Harley to help divert traffic into the openings in the yard. Suddenly, a car loomed in front of me! He had

While 1948 saw the first Panhead, it was not ordered for this St. Louis PD motor. This officer rides a 74 side valve with a right-hand shifter. It is radio equipped and has a foot-operated siren. The luggage carrier has an unusual zippered bag for either the officer's extra gear or a first-aid kit. *St. Louis, Missouri, Police Dept. Archives*

The motor on the left is a 1940 model 80. Under the rider's seat is a flashlight, attached to the frame. The headlight has a chrome visor, and there is a small chrome flying goose on the top of the front fender. The two officers appear to be displaying some type of first-aid equipment. The motor on the right is an Indian of the same era. *Corpus Christi, Texas, Police Archives*

worked his way through seven lanes to get out of the shipyard. I hit him right at the hood, and then literally flew over him. I'll never know why I didn't leave some essential parts behind! I lit on my hands and back, rolled over twice and got up. No broken bones, no nothing—except scared shoeless!

"With four sets of strong arms, we pulled my front wheel back from the frame of my motor, so I could get back to the city garage."

In response to an article appearing in *Smithsonian* magazine concerning the Harley-Davidson motorcycle, Roderick G. Welsh wrote this letter to the editor, which was printed in the January 1994 issue.

Dear Sir:

I rode Harley Hogs for 25 years in the Long Beach Police Department and can refute your statement that 100mph was tops for a stock Hog.

On patrol one day in 1941, a hopped-up hot rod went through a stop sign at about 50mph. I took chase, red lights and siren on. The driver leaned out of the car and waved for me to come on after him. I said to myself, "I'll get you if I have to chase you till I run out of gas." I had sport bars and no windshield, so I flattened out like a jockey, with only my eyes showing over the headlight. I got 102mph out of old 828, my model 61 Hog.

After a wild chase the hot rodder pulled up on the wrong side of the street in front of a hospital. He jumped out and said, 'My dad is being operated on and needs blood.' With gun drawn, I said, 'I've heard every excuse but that one. Let's find out if you're lying.' It was true. We both had our blood tested, and, thank heaven, his matched. I told him good-bye and good luck...no ticket.

And finally, we close out the forties with another of Roderick G. Welsh's stories, called "Slide Rod, Slide."

"One, hot summer day, I decided to work the ocean side of Long Beach. Our uniforms were hot—they were made of wool—so I was parked by the bluff, cooling off. Then 'swoosh'...what I was being paid for sped by. Out I go after him.

"At that point, there was a fork in the road. The left fork stayed next to the coast and the right fork went to Belmont Shores. I wanted to find out which road he was going to take.

This 1942 photo shows a unique combination of Harleys. The Corpus Christi motor officer (second from right) rides a 1940 Harley. The other motor officers are members of the U.S. Navy Shore Patrol. They also ride Harleys of 1941 or 1942 vintage. The pursuit light configuration is slightly different on each motorcycle. The motor on the left appears to have an electric siren mounted on the front fender. While the military typically ordered its own variation (WLA models), these Navy men appear to be riding standard Harleys. The two Naval officers on either side of the city police officer were former motor officers with the Corpus Christi Police Department. *Corpus Christi, Texas, Police Archives*

He indicated he was following the coast, so I pulled up on his blind side. Suddenly, he changed his mind and swerved to the right. I was trapped. The upshot was that my cycle slid past him on the left, and I slid past him on the right. I measured my body slide on the asphalt to be 119 feet!

"I left all the leather on my gloves and the knees of my pants, and between my hands and knees, left about a square foot of skin on the asphalt. My iron horse needed a new paint job, and I needed a big box of Band-Aids. The man I stopped was very solicitous, saying that it was all his fault, and that he'd have his insurance company contact me. They did! I got new gloves, pants, glasses, and shirt. But, dumb me, I didn't charge them for my precious skin!"

LEFT
While Ofc. Jack Wallace of the Charlotte Police Department smiles at the camera, a sedan speeds past. Officer Wallace rides a war year (1941–1946) Harley painted black. War year Harleys varied in detail and appearance due to shortages of critically needed defense materials. This motorcycle has bright wheel rims while most of the era had painted rims. Without a radio, the space on each side of the rear wheel is effectively used with the addition of a set of Harley accessory saddlebags. *Charlotte-Mecklenburg (North Carolina) Police Dept. Archives*

The deep fins on the heads of this 1941–1946 Harley reveal it as an 80ci side-valve motor. A radio receiver, a pair of red pursuit lights, and fender placard have been added. *Richmond, Virginia, Police Dept. Archives*

1948, Chicago; one of those great group photos
police departments did years ago. The two rows
of cars are 1948 Ford coupes and sedans. The
solo motorcycles are new Panheads with a long
line of Servi-Cars in front. *Harley-Davidson Archives*

In March 1942 the Hammond (Indiana) Police Department took delivery of these five new 74 OHV Harleys. This photo shows the large "barn doors" or "bat wings," as the early fairings were called. The material was a rubber covered canvas. Leg shields were available, but not installed on these motors. *Harley-Davidson Archives*

A June 1944 photo of Honolulu's motor squad. If you look carefully, you can see the blackout headlight covers, a wartime requirement. *Harley-Davidson Archives*

RIGHT
1948 saw the introduction of the Panhead motor. It replaced the Knucklehead and was offered in two ci versions (61ci and 74ci) like its predecessor. The 1948 model was unique as it was the first year for a new engine and the last for the springer front suspension. *Harley-Davidson Archives*

ABOVE
The unique shape of the rocker covers is why this engine (74ci OHV) is called a Knucklehead. The Knucklehead was produced in two (61ci and 74ci) versions between 1936 and 1947. The introduction of this powerful motor was beset with lubrication problems. Within a year, those problems were resolved. This particular motorcycle is a 1947 police model with radio, first-aid kit, fire extinguisher, pursuit lights, and front fender "Police" placard. *Harley-Davidson Archives*

NEXT PAGE TOP
His first day on the job as a motor officer for the Los Angeles Police Department was a big thrill for Bob Hale, who had dreamed of riding motors since boyhood. His first bike was this 1947 Knucklehead, Unit No. 502, which his fellow motor officers called "the drunk motorcycle." The code violation number in California for "driving while under the influence of alcohol" was 502. Officer Hale rode approximately 250,000 miles of Los Angeles city pavement on Harley-Davidson motorcycles during his eighteen-year stint on motors. Although he retired from the LAPD in 1968, Hale still rides a Harley today. *Bob Hale Collection*

NEXT PAGE BOTTOM
1941 through 1946 carried the same tank trim consisting of an emblem and a horizontal stainless band that extended from each end. The fenders were assembled from three pieces: a center section and a valence panel spot-welded to each side. The row of welds is covered with a bright strip. The crossbar mounted lights were a Harley option. The handgrip on the left handlebar is for the front brake. When a front fender "Police" placard is ordered, the front fender light is deleted, thus the two holes. *Harley-Davidson Archives*

NEXT PAGES RIGHT
1944 photo shows two very clean Minneapolis, Minnesota, Police solo motors ridden by two happy motor cops, Ofc. Robert Bullock (left) and Sgt. Clair Tripp. Between the two of them, they have logged over 500,000 miles and each have twenty years of service as police motorcycle officers. With shortages of materials during the war years (1941–1946), they were probably pleased to have new motors. Both bikes have fork-mounted pursuit lights. At the time this photo was taken, the Minneapolis Police Department was using Harley-Davidsons exclusively. *Harley-Davidson Archives*

This Harley studio shot of a 1941–1946 model 80 shows typical police accessories offered. Front and rear safety guards were painted black. The model's footwear is enhanced with a pair of puttees. *Harley-Davidson Archives*

Seventeen Harleys belonging to the Long Beach (California) Police Department Drill Team lead a parade down Ocean Boulevard. After their participation in the parade, they broke off for traffic control. *Roderick G. Welsh Collection*

ABOVE
Long Beach (California) Motor Patrol Association decal from 1944. *Roderick G. Welsh Collection*

RIGHT
Sgt. Roderick G. Welsh of the Long Beach (California) Police Motor Squad sits on a 1941 model 61 Knucklehead. *Roderick G. Welsh Collection*

A 1948 model 74 side-valve engine. The bike has a radio receiver mounted on the rear luggage rack. The radio speaker and framework for the bat wings are clearly shown in the side view. While many officers used sheepskin for a seat cover, this motor has a simple cover, probably of leather. Rear safety bars are painted, and the front bars are chrome. *Richmond, Virginia, Police Dept. Archives*

Many of the designs created by Harley-Davidson
stylists were considered works of art like the
siren on this 1941–1946. The flowing lines of the
siren are beautifully integrated into the shape of
the frame. The tooled, leather saddlebags are
classic Harley. Marring the lovely lines is a
functional, riveted metal rack on the rear
fender. *Harley-Davidson Archives*

CHAPTER 6

The Fifties: Post-War Boom

The fifties were good years for Harley-Davidson. The most important innovation for the fifties motorcycle was Harley's introduction of the Duo-Glide in 1958. Of particular interest to police motor officers, hydraulic rear suspension offered a more stable and comfortable ride for those long shifts running traffic. The hydraulic rear brake was a safety feature for motor officers who needed a more reliable braking system. Hydraulic rear brakes were also offered on the Servi-Car, still very much in use by police agencies for parking enforcement.

Harley-Davidson celebrated its fifty year anniversary, and added a brass medallion to all 1954 models. Although by now Indian was out of the motorcycle business, inexpensive foreign-made motorcycles had already invaded the civilian market.

1952 was the first year for the foot shift on the big twin. This Islip, New York, patrolman looks happy with his new Harley. By the early fifties, most departments had radios on their motorcycles, although there is none on this one. *Suffolk County Police Museum*

Cincinnati Police Department

In 1950, there were twenty-two solo motorcycles and eight Servi-Cars in use in the Cincinnati Police Department. Two of the Servi-Cars were assigned to two outlying districts to assist with traffic enforcement. The rest of the motorcycle fleet remained in the Highway Safety Bureau and was used for selective enforcement as needed.

In 1954, Police Chief Stanley Schrotel saw the need for more training and started the "Police Training Road Run" as an experiment of in-service training for motor officers. The run was designed to test the skills of the riders, giving them experience in negotiating unusual road surfaces such as brick, cobblestone, railroad, and streetcar tracks. Rather than a speed race, this was a training exercise. Any rider who reached designated checkpoints too early had his scores penalized for riding too fast.

For the first time, all of Cincinnati's motorcycles were equipped with two-way radios.

The solo motorcycles were used for accident investigation and calls for quick response, as well as for general police patrol. In 1957, helmets were issued to all solo motorcycle patrolmen (CHP motor officers were also issued helmets that year). Servi-cars were assigned as needed for traffic enforcement according to accident rates, traffic congestion, and crime levels. In 1958, officers operating the Servi-Cars won first place in a national safety contest conducted by the National Safety Council. Members were credited with more than one year of accident free operation.

Dallas Police Department

The February 1957 issue of *Motorcyclist* magazine featured an article about the Dallas Police Motorcycle Brigade, which was the largest police motor squad in the Southwest. The addi-

Officer Ed Turner of the Mobile Police Department pauses from his busy day to have his photo taken with his son. His motorcycle is a 1950 74ci Panhead. It is interesting to note that this motorcycle has no radio and no saddlebags for storage. *Mobile, Alabama, Police Archives*

tion of twelve rookie motor officers that year brought the number of solo units to fifty-two. Prior to World War II, the squad enjoyed an excellent reputation. But during the war, the unit lacked qualified personnel and was eventually disbanded except for six motorcycles that were used for escort duties.

The Dallas brigade was divided into four platoons that patrolled city traffic on a twenty-hour daily operation. The brigade also provided a free escort service for funeral processions. But the duties of traffic enforcement were their primary concerns. Statistics showed that among the total number of traffic violators

apprehended, the greatest percentage of arrests were made by motor officers. Although speeders, drunk drivers, and other traffic violators were the main targets of motor officers, their activities often helped solve other crimes of a more serious nature. Routine traffic stops could result in the apprehension of a suspect wanted on another outstanding warrant. And the maneuverability of the motorcycle often resulted in catching a suspect fleeing the scene of a crime. The presence and appearance of an officer on a motorcycle commanded respect, especially from teenagers.

In 1954, members of the Dallas Motorcycle Brigade became one of the first police departments in the nation to be issued fiber crash helmets. The helmets greatly reduced head injuries in the department and soon became standard equipment for police motor officers nationwide.

In 1953, Harley-Davidson offered two different 74ci Panhead motors: a standard, high-compression engine and a low-compression engine with unique cam and carburetion for city police use. There was also a city gearing option for low-speed riding. *Orlando, Florida, Police Archives*

Orlando Police Department

The following information was gleaned from the November/December 1958 issue of the *Florida Police Journal*, the official publication of the Florida Peace Officers' Association. The article highlights the progress of the Orlando Police Department under Chief Johnstone.

In 1958, the Orlando Police Department operated under three bureaus: The Uniformed Bureau, Administrative Bureau, and Detective Bureau. The training school fell directly under the supervision of the Chief of Police, Carlisle Johnstone.

The Uniformed Bureau was responsible for adequate and systematic patrol of the city

A St. Louis Police Department mechanic is about to balance the front wheel of a new, early fifties Panhead. *St. Louis, Missouri, Police Archives*

to prevent crime and other disorders. They were also responsible for enforcing all traffic lanes and for the apprehension of violators

The owner of the 1958 Plymouth convertible doesn't look too happy about his ticket. The Harley appears to be a 1954, but lacks the Fiftieth Anniversary fender emblem. The mid-fifties saw the first use of helmets by motor officers. The shape and markings of this officer's headgear are rather unique. *Orlando, Florida, Police Archives*

during or immediately after the commission of a crime.

The duties of the Uniformed Bureau were divided into foot patrol, squad car, and motorcycle patrol. Five meter maids rode three-wheel motors, Harley-Davidson Servi-Cars. The motor officers were assigned on two shifts, riding ten Harleys, from 7:00 a.m. to 10:00 p.m.

The photos in the Florida Police Journal show the men mounted on their Harleys, wearing dark, long-sleeved shirts, ties, tan breeches, leather boots, and partial helmets with small sun visors. All motorcycles had the wind screen. The meter maids wore the same long-sleeved dark

This 1954 FL of the Royal Canadian Mounted Police is radio equipped. Large storage boxes have been added above the radio boxes. *RCMP Archives*

This young lad is no doubt having the time of his life sitting on his dad's new 1954 Fiftieth Anniversary Harley. Two-way radios were available from Harley at a list price of over $600, more than half the cost of the motorcycle. *Bob Hale Collection*

shirts and ties, but wore tan slacks and soft caps. The Servi-Cars all had wind screens.

V-Twin Tales: Harleys on Patrol

Motor Officer John I. "Jack" Stoner

Ofc. John I. "Jack" Stoner began riding for the Salt Lake City (Utah) Police Department in 1958 on a 1956 Harley. The motor had a rigid frame with radios on the back in metal boxes. The boxes were painted black and measured about 24in by 10in by 8in. You had to continue riding to keep the battery charged, otherwise it would be dead within two hours and you would

be on "receive only." If dispatch needed you, they would have to wait about ninety seconds for you to turn the transistor on and warm up the console. There was no place to carry anything. You kept your ticket book in the inside pocket of your leather jacket.

The motorcycle had a rigid frame and a front mount Motorola transistor weighing about thirty to forty pounds. It was mounted to the front handlebars, and everything was okay as long as you were doing at least 20 to 25mph; any slower and they would fall over due to the poor weight distribution. You were always fighting the front end even though the bike had a front shock damper that you could loosen or tighten.

One day Ofc. Stoner was chasing a dump truck. The truck made it across the railroad tracks as a train passed by. Unable to make it through, Ofc. Stoner sped ahead to beat the train to the next crossing. He crossed

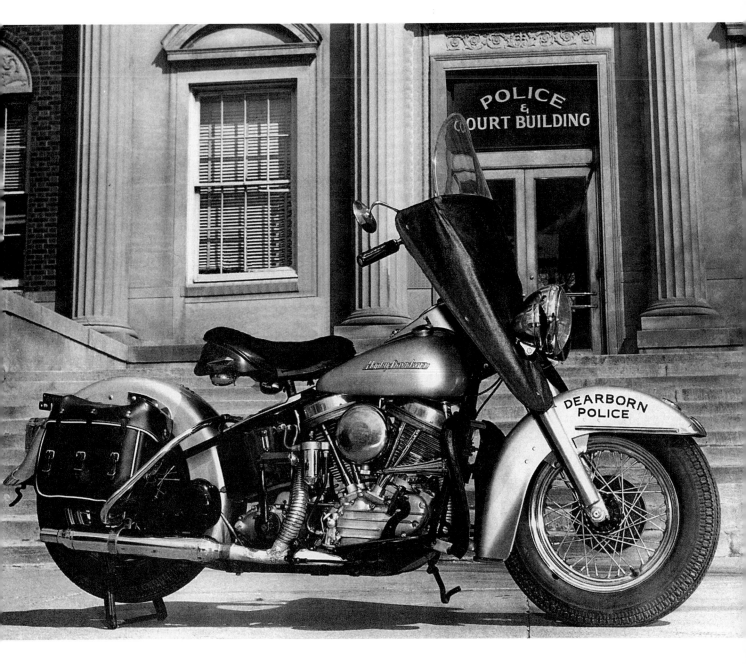

The 1954 Harley-Davidson motorcycles all carried a special Fiftieth Anniversary medallion on the front fender. The list price for this 74ci Panhead was $1,015. An option called "Deluxe Group," consisting of additional chrome parts, was added to this motorcycle at a cost of $75.75. *Dearborn Historical Society*

the tracks at an angle and landed in the rutted road. When the unsprung rear end of the Harley hit the road, it bent the axle, sending the rear wheel above his head. As he was flying end-over-end through the air, he recalled thinking to himself, "You keep screwin' around, Jack, and you're gonna wreck this bike." The handlebar broke off, the helmet split, and some ribs were broken, but he continued to ride until the next accident, at which point it would be time to do something else!

Then there was the siren on the front wheel. "You're going down the street on a code-three (emergency response)," Stoner recalled, "and that siren is starting to wind up. When that thing hit a pitch, all of a sudden you couldn't focus your eyes! It was bedlam. The pitch of this siren was so intense, you couldn't see, hear, or think. It was better to have the siren on the back wheel, but you had to step on it to get it going if the frame was bent or if there had been a change in tire pressure."

Funeral escort was a regular duty of motor officers. In this case, the escort was for one of their own. Sgt. Robert Dula, was killed on April 8, 1955, by a hit-and-run driver, and was the first motor officer killed in the line of duty for the Las Vegas Police Department. *Las Vegas Police Archives*

The biggest hazards to motor officers were railroad tracks, big dogs, and snow. There were no thermal suits then, Stoner recalled. "You got a squad car when your knees got numb." Today, motor officers in Salt Lake City are issued standard snowmobile suits and are expected to ride in cold winter weather as long as the roads are dry.

Motor Officer Rod Welsh

Rod Welsh rode motors for the Long Beach (California) Police Department from 1937 to 1951. He has kept written journals of his "war stories," including this one entitled, "Rod and the Hilltoppers".

Surrounded by the city of Long Beach is a small city by the name of Signal Hill, which is also the highest point in the area. In the 1800s, Sepulveda and Dominguez Rancho owners would sight a cargo ship off the coast and build a roaring fire to indicate they had cowhides for sale.

In this interesting city was a motorcycle club called the Hilltoppers. It was a good club, unlike the Hell's Angels you hear so much about. We motor officers and the Hilltoppers got along fine. We even attended their meetings and gave them safety tips.

One day, one of the younger Hilltoppers spotted me and 'raced' his motor. This meant, 'Let's race.' Or in this case, 'Try and catch me.' I accepted his challenge. We went up one street and down an-

In the mid-fifties there was a prevailing fear of a nuclear attack. Schools conducted periodic air-raid drills and civil defense workers were given gas masks for protection. Bell, California, Police Motor Officer John Senter puts on his mask for the photo while sitting on his Fiftieth Anniversary Harley-Davidson. The OHV emblem is on the side of the front fender, with the Fiftieth Anniversary medallion on top. *Bell, California, Police Archives*

other, all over the hill, dotted with oil derricks, and down around the wells. This lasted about half an hour. I thought, enough is enough, so I trapped him into a dead-end street where he finally stopped.

I didn't write him a speeding ticket, but cited him for reckless driving. Still, we parted friends. I don't know what it cost him in court, but I was told later by a member of the club that whatever it was, it didn't compare with what he got from them.

The beautiful tank emblem that graced the sides of the 1955 and 1956 models. *Harley-Davidson Archives*

A studio model sits proudly on a 1956 FL. He wears the motor officer uniform of the day, which includes this Garrison-style hat. *Harley-Davidson Archives*

I enjoyed the chase. It was fun matching riding skills with a 'hot dog.' It just goes to prove that a Harley Hog in the hands of an old-timer is superior to a lighter machine ridden by one less skilled. Made me feel like a kid again!

Sgt. John Skelton looks with pride at his traffic
officers on their Harleys. With one exception, all
are fitted with their winter bat wings for this
photo taken in December 1956. *Las Vegas Police
Archives*

A 1957 FLH; the last of the big Harleys with an unsprung rear wheel, commonly called a "hard tail." The large box on the side of the rear wheel is the radio transmitter. The receiver is mounted on the right side. Both of these units were shock mounted with rubber isolators. Although the azaleas were blooming, the weather was still cold enough for Ofc. Sherman Blackwell to keep the leg shields on his motorcycle. *Mobile, Alabama, Police Archives*

LEFT
Two brand-new 1957 vehicles of the Royal
Canadian Mounted Police: a Ford sedan and a
Harley FLH. There is no radio installed on this
motorcycle, just a beautiful set of saddlebags.
Notice the lanyard around the officer's neck
leading to his revolver. A positive method of
weapon retention. *RCMP Archives*

ABOVE
Five Royal Canadian Mounted Police Harleys of
mid-fifties vintage motor along. *RCMP Archives*

RIGHT
Harley offered a fire extinguisher as a police
option. These extinguishers were the
carbontetrachloride and water variety, and were
manufactured by the Pyrene Company of
Newark, New Jersey. Mounts varied between
handlebars, luggage rack, or side mount, as
shown here. These extinguishers were not very
durable, tended to leak, and often failed to
work when needed. *Harley-Davidson Archives*

A cutaway view of the Panhead motor, so named
for the shape of the stamped rocker covers.
Harley-Davidson Archives

*Holiday or week-end motorists
snarl up your traffic flow?*

See how you can shift traffic
control officers to cope with
jams before they develop...
with exceptionally mobile,
HARLEY-DAVIDSON
SOLOS

COME summer, many intersections that would
normally require only arterial control can
periodically become dangerous bottlenecks.
   But when you have plenty of men mounted on
radio-dispatched Harley-Davidson Solos, you can
shift forces to meet changing traffic patterns. What's
more, Solos have the speed and acceleration to
pursue and apprehend offenders. Overall result —
smoother traffic flow...few accidents and fatalities.
   See your dealer now or write for details. HARLEY-
DAVIDSON MOTOR CO., Milwaukee 1, Wisconsin.

*Tips to more effective
use of police manpower*

This free booklet shows how and why leading communities are getting "more effective
round-the-clock police power" with Harley-
Davidson police motorcycles. Send for your copy.

HARLEY-DAVIDSON police motorcycles

RIGHT
**A 1957 advertisement for Harley-Davidson solo
motorcycles.** *Harley-Davidson Archives*

Located behind the 74ci Panhead engine and below the seat is the large capacity oil tank, offered as an option for police use. The triangular-shaped box in front of the rear wheel shock absorber is the tool kit. *Harley-Davidson Archives*

Factory photo showing a birch-white 1958 Police FL. It's equipped with a two-way Motorola radio and front wheel siren. In 1958, Harley offered chrome rims, chrome safety guards, and chrome mufflers as options (not pictured here). *Harley-Davidson Archives*

CHP MEMORIES

California Highway Patrol Archives

Caption under this photo, which appeared in the 1956 *Bakersfield Californian*, read: Snappy new safety helmets for the California Highway Patrol are exhibited by these four Kern County highway patrolmen. From left to right are Lt. William K. Earl and Traffic Officers Gene Phillips, Don Bianchi and Fred Brown.

BELOW
A November 1958 photo of the Las Vegas Police shows an all-Harley motor squad. *Las Vegas Police Archives*

This 1957 FL was number 0001 when delivered to the St. Louis Police Department. After two years of service, it was purchased by a motor officer and ridden for thirty-one years. It was recently restored to its original glory by Dale Walksler, a Harley-Davidson dealer in Mount Vernon, Illinois. *Dale Walksler Collection*

CHAPTER 7

The Sixties: More Horsepower and Electric Start

The introduction in 1965 of the electric starter was big news for police motor officers. The addition of the Electra-Glide into police fleets improved the getaway time for motor officers in a hurry. It was also in 1965 that Harley-Davidson introduced a twelve-volt electrical system. Police agency purchasers were instructed to get a conversion kit from Motorola to make older, six-volt radios compatible with the new model. Beginning in 1966, purchasers were informed that all radios and radio equipment would have to be ordered direct from the manufacturer. In 1966, the Electra-Glide received an increase in horsepower of between ten and fifteen percent with the introduction of the Shovelhead motor. A motor officer can never have too much power.

The California Highway Patrol

In 1960, the California Highway Patrol developed a new motorcycle training program. All cadets went through a basic course, but motor officers went through an advanced course before going out into the field on their motors. Also in 1960, officers riding motorcycles were given bonus pay for this type of duty. By 1963, the CHP's vehicle fleet included 433 motorcycles. In 1969, CHP motor officers were given jurisdiction over the Los Angeles freeway system.

A 1961 Duo-Glide with a rotating beacon extended to its maximum length, as it would be displayed in a traffic control situation with the motorcycle parked. *Harley-Davidson Archives*

Cincinnati Police Department: A Thirty-Year Hiatus Begins

On October 13, 1961, the solo motorcycles were discontinued in Cincinnati. The solo was replaced with high-performance automobiles. This change resulted in greater safety to the operator and increased the number of vehicles available for use in all weather conditions. The expansion of the expressway system was the rea-

A 1961 Duo-Glide with a fork-mounted rotating beacon. *Tampa, Florida, Police Archives*

son for the change away from motorcycles. The Police Division continued to use Servi-Cars for accident investigation and traffic enforcement on surface streets throughout the remainder of the sixties. It would be another thirty years before the Cincinnati Police Department took delivery of a two-wheel Harley-Davidson motorcycle for police work.

V-Twin Tales: Harleys on Patrol

Motor Officer Dick Tush

Dick Tush began riding motors for the San Jose Police Department in 1969 at the age of thirty-three. He had never ridden a motorcycle until he climbed onto the department's 1967 Harley-Davidson. When he came home with the motorcycle, his wife was shocked, thinking he was going to ride three-wheelers, not two-wheel-

ers. Her attitude changed upon hearing that the job entailed getting an additional $40 per month in wages. In those days, training consisted of about three days with a sergeant who showed you the ropes. Then, you learned through experience and by asking other motor officers to give you tips on how to maneuver. In 1971, the department began sending officers to the CHP motor training course, and it wasn't until he had completed the course that Ofc. Tush truly felt comfortable and safe on the motorcycle.

Ofc. Tush remembers a CHP sergeant at the academy who sat on his Harley as if he had been assembled onto it at the factory as part of the unit. He "looked just like Cochise," the Apache chief, sitting up on the hill astride his Harley. He was at one with his motorcycle, the same way a cowboy is at one with his horse. This sensation of being part of the machine is critical to a rider's performance and overall safety. With the old Harleys, when you got comfortable in that saddle, you could "make that mother scoot."

In the summer of 1961, the Omaha Police motor squad pose for this photo outside their department garage. *Omaha, Nebraska, Police Archives*

But sometimes those Harleys didn't stop like you thought they should. Ofc. Tush was having a "turtle race" one day with another officer. In a turtle race, two riders go from point A to point B as slowly as possible without putting a foot down and without falling. Then you race back to point A. On this particular day, he didn't have any brakes as he sped back to point A, and he ended up hitting something in order to stop. The tricky part was explaining to the Accident Review Board how he bent his forks on a railroad track during a turtle race!

Because he was a speeder himself, Ofc. Tush liked to work speeders. He worked the surface streets and boulevards in places where he knew people would open it up a little bit. Commuters used side streets to circumvent traffic during morning rush. They would zoom down two lane residential streets in excess of the speed limit, and that's where they would get nailed. "When you're shaggin' a speeder," Tush explained, "Your 'radar' is out. You're trying to hide, stay in the blind spot, but you're watching side streets, brake lights, and careless drivers."

Working drunk drivers was interesting, too. It didn't take long to spot one. One evening,

Ofc. Tush and another motor officer were sitting in a restaurant, completing the paperwork on the five drunk drivers they had arrested during that shift. Ofc. Tush looked out the restaurant window, and spotted yet another drunk. With an elbow to his partner, they took off after him. Upon their return, they now had paperwork to do on the sixth drunk driver for the evening. But then, he wondered, how would he write the report? "I was sitting in a booth at Original Joe's Restaurant having a cup of coffee, when I happened to look out the window...."

Ofc. Tush had few complaints about the Harley-Davidson motorcycle. In fact, four years after his retirement in 1988, he bought a cream and black Heritage Softail that reminds him of his first motor. In those days, he recalled, the corporation had a take-it-or-leave-it attitude with police departments. "They weren't responsive to the motor officer's suggestions and were reluctant to change the machine unless they had to. Harley didn't come out with an electric start until Honda did. The kick start seemed like a macho thing, but when you're a motor officer, you want to get on and go, now!"

Today, you can't get Dick Tush off his Harley. If it's not raining, that's where you'll find him. He says it's ironic to have started riding Harleys for the first time as a police officer and to

ABOVE AND BELOW
A 1961 Sportster, which was an engineering exercise at Harley-Davidson. The company took a black XLH and added a few police accessories. Although some departments may have used Sportsters during this time, Harley never officially offered this optional equipment.
Harley-Davidson Archives

resume riding one in retirement. To explain this, he paraphrases a philosopher who wrote, "The end of all our travels will be where we start; and we will see the place for the first time."

Captain John Welter and Lieutenant William Brown
    Capt. John Welter and Lt. William Brown of the San Diego Police Department recall that being a motor officer was a prestigious and sought after assignment. Most guys would have done anything to ride motors. Some experience was preferred, but you couldn't have any bad habits. They were looking for people with natural ability.
    Most of the training was slow speed drills. The clutch was a killer. The training was not fun and was particularly difficult for those with no riding experience. The training lasted for two weeks. You spent the first day in the classroom, the last day on a two-hundred-mile ride, with everything in between being slow-speed cone drills. In training, you had to keep both feet on the footboards. It doesn't look cool to have your legs flailing around in the air or dragging on the ground. A good rider can do the drills sitting sidesaddle.
    A new motor officer was paired with an experienced rider for about a week. The experienced

Two Milwaukee officers with their brand-new, 1962 Harleys: one a Duo-Glide solo and the other a Servi-Car. *Harley-Davidson Archives*

officer would show the new officer how to overtake a car, avoid a vehicle's blind spot, and ride in formation. The officer on the left usually set the pace. It was best to ride side by side, since it wasn't cool to stagger. In those days, the CHP taught new officers how to lay the bike down. Guys who had experience riding dirt bikes really knew how to handle a sliding bike. It took about three years of riding to be considered a good rider.

On one particular day, Ofc. Brown had just finished writing a parking ticket. He hopped on his Harley, took off, and immediately put his feet on the footboards. A slow turn around a parked car, and he gassed it. Unfortunately, Harleys couldn't take a lot of throttle at slow speed; the motor backfired and died. Immediately, Ofc. Brown's legs began to flail as he lost

his balance. The bike went down in two stages: first the crash bar, then the handlebars. As he leaped away on one foot from the falling Harley, a tourist approached him asking for directions. Unflappable, Ofc. Brown walked over to the tourist, his demeanor indicating that he meant to park the bike that way. Although the tank was leaking fuel, he took his time giving directions, not once losing his "motor officer cool."

Most officers you talk to would admit to having dropped their motorcycle at least once, breaking a light in the process. The most logical thing to do was to sneak into the garage and "borrow" a light off another bike. Otherwise, your incident of dropping the bike would be considered a traffic accident, for which you would get a one-day suspension.

As everyone knows, old Harleys have their own little idiosyncrasies. First, you couldn't gas it without causing the motor to cough. Another quirk was the backfire. If you had an ounce of decency as a prankster, you would sneak up on a fellow officer, ride in his blind spot, and allow him to experience the pleasure of the unexpected backfire. First, you would turn off your switch above 20mph and pump it a few times. Then, you would turn the switch back on and scare the living daylights out of the guy with your backfire. Stalling was common, as well. If you were riding in a parade, you were constantly working the clutch to avoid toppling over before throngs of spectators.

You could always tell who the Harley riders were. All you had to do was look for the big stain just above the right boot top where the carburetor leaked onto the kick lever. That lever vibrated around, getting the pants dirty. The Harley was lower to the ground and felt heavier and more stable. It was a great image bike, but the vibration tended to loosen parts.

The siren was foot-operated in those days and had to be adjusted to compensate for tire wear. Sometimes at freeway speed, a new tire expanded, setting off the siren unexpectedly. You would have to stuff your boot into the siren to keep it from spinning until you could get it adjusted! One guy wore horseshoe cleats on his boot heels. It was easier to stuff the cleated heel into the siren to stop it from going off. Another benefit of cleated boots was that you made a lot of noise walking down the halls of the courthouse. And while riding your motorcycle at night, you could let your feet drag on the ground, creating a big shower of sparks to impress the kids!

Your bike was inspected every day. Everyone in the family got to clean the bike.

Police Headquarters in Mobile is located at 51 Government Street. In June 1962, the officers gather for inspection. Both Servi-Car and solo motor officers wore helmets. *Mobile, Alabama, Police Archives*

And every two weeks you would steam clean it. Lemon Pledge™ was a good cleaner, but it attracted bees. Another occasional hazard was bees in your helmet.

By the early sixties, motor officers of the Royal Canadian Mounted Police were wearing helmets. *RCMP Archives*

Police Chief Don Rheam

Police Chief Don Rheam of the Anderson (Indiana) Police Department has a collection of great stories from his years riding three-wheel and two-wheel Harley-Davidson motorcycles. The one he likes the best occurred on June 11, 1969, when he was riding a 1964 Harley:

I was approaching an intersection and began to lean into a turn when I hit an oil slick and laid down the cycle. I escaped all injuries except for breaking my canister of chemical mace located on my gun belt. Not realizing at first that the canister had broken, an officer following me ran to my aid, removed the canister and threw it from harm's way. I was taken to the hospital, checked, and released.

I had already been scheduled to escort the funeral procession for a retired officer and had to leave immediately. As a result, I didn't have time to change out of my uniform. Al-

The Charlotte Police motor officers are suited up in their dress uniforms, complete with white gloves, for this 1962 Thanksgiving Day Parade. *Charlotte-Mecklenburg, North Carolina, Police Archives*

though the mace had saturated a portion of my uniform, I was immune to the fumes by the time I arrived at the funeral.

The deceased officer had been retired for several years and did not have any close police friends remaining. Very few of our current officers personally knew the deceased, but out of respect for a retired brother officer, a large gathering of officers attended the funeral.

I went in and sat down with my fellow officers. As I looked around, I noticed many of the officers were wiping tears from their eyes. Family members and others in attendance were quite amazed at how emotional all of the police officers were, unaware that they were all merely reacting to the mace fumes still lingering on my uniform! This story is still being told twenty-five years later.

The dominance of Harley-Davidson over the police motorcycle market would soon be challenged in ways as yet unimagined. Soon, the foreign-made motorcycle would begin to count police agencies among its new customers.

This mid-sixties photo of the Tampa Police Motor Squad shows a mix of Duo-Glides and Electra-Glides. *Tampa, Florida, Police Archives*

These Omaha Police motor officers gather in the department garage, wearing their dress uniforms, either for an inspection or for a special event, such as a parade. *Omaha, Nebraska, Police Archives*

RIGHT
Ofc. Robert Hoagland is not smiling because this was the last day of the Charlotte Police motor squad. Soon after this photo was taken, Hoagland's 1965 FLB was sold. 1965 was the first year for the electric starter, and the last for the Panhead motor. Note the interesting exhaust pipe extension. *Charlotte-Mecklenburg, North Carolina, Police Archives*

ABOVE AND RIGHT
Two detail shots of rear wheel sirens on 1963–65 Electra-Glides. To activate the siren, the officer depressed the lever with the heel of his left boot. The siren pivoted on its mount and the shaft made contact with the tire, thereby spinning the siren. Depressing and releasing the lever produced the siren "wail." The coil spring on the cable limited the amount of force an officer could apply. Rear wheel sirens were preferred over front-mounted siren, because the noise level was lower in the rear. In addition, sirens were known to explode from time to time. Rear wheel sirens suffered in colder climates from the accumulation of ice and road grime and could freeze solid. *Harley-Davidson Archives*

In 1964, a Kidde dry chemical extinguisher was available in addition to the Pyrene fire extinguisher. The chemical extinguisher mounted horizontally on the rear fender behind the seat. A metal first-aid kit mounted on top of the fender. *Harley-Davidson Archives*

A birch-white 1964 Panhead with black plastic saddlebags. *Harley-Davidson Archives*

ABOVE
Clark County Motor Officers Jim McGuire and Chuck Smith with their black-and-white 1964 Duo-Glides. Note the unique drive-off stand on the motor on the right. *Las Vegas, Nevada, Police Archives*

BELOW
Eleven black-and-white Electra-Glides outside the Clark County Sheriff's Office in June 1969. *Las Vegas, Nevada, Police Archives*

Police departments often held competitions between motor officers to sharpen skills. The year is 1968, and the officer closest to the camera rides a 1964 Duo-Glide. In the background, Officer James V. Heyden sits astride a foot-shift Electra-Glide. Officer Heyden won the competition for that year. He retired in 1994 after thirty-three years with the Lansing (Michigan) Police Department. *Patricia Heyden Collection*

Two motor officers pose with the pilots from the U.S. Air Force precision flying team, the Thunderbirds. Their black-and-white Electra-Glides (circa 1965) are radio equipped. *Ogden, Utah, Police Archives*

The Corpus Christi Police motor unit lines up its motors for this 1961 photo. The solos are a combination of 1959 to 1961 Duo-Glides. At the far right is a solitary Servi-Car. *Corpus Christi, Texas, Police Archives*

RIGHT
In 1966, Harley-Davidson introduced the first Shovelhead. This spotless motorcycle was assigned to the Salt Lake City Police Department. *Salt Lake City, Utah, Police Archives*

CHAPTER 8

The Seventies and Eighties: Quality Lost, and Found

Beginning in the early seventies, the dominance of Harley-Davidson over the police market was threatened. In 1972, the California Highway Patrol, with its long tradition of Harley use, tested a fleet of fifteen Honda 750s and fifteen Moto Guzzi 850s. In 1975, however, the CHP purchased 130 Kawasaki 900s for road patrol. Although Harley had been the official choice of the CHP since 1933, bids were now open for the first time to both Harley and Kawasaki, with the department purchasing from the lowest bidder. In 1977, the popular television series, "CHiPs," began, featuring actors riding Kawasakis. Today, some motor officers joke that if actor Erik Estrada had been riding a Harley, he'd still be on television! But that's another story.

The Seventies

A number of things happened almost simultaneously, resulting in a shift away from Harley by some police agencies. What happened to Harley's civilian touring bike market happened, by default, to police bikes as well. And the corporate struggles of Harley-Davidson were inevitably manifest in the motorcycles offered to police agencies.

Japanese manufacturers had been developing larger bikes, with better performance at lower cost, in anticipation of satisfying a demand that had been steadily growing. It was precisely this strategy that enabled the Japanese manufacturers to penetrate the passenger vehicle market, as well. Big Harleys were by now infamous for leaking oil and breaking down. If given a choice, why

Maneuvering up and down the hills of San Francisco on a motorcycle is a challenge. A seven-point star bearing the initials "S.F.P.D." is on the side of the tank on this 1978 Harley. Mounted vertically behind the right fork is the officer's baton. *Michael Kan Collection*

wouldn't the consumer, including a police department, pick what was perceived to be a superior product?

In 1975, Kawasaki took serious aim at the police market. They went to the user and asked,

125

In the mid-seventies, Harley police motors were given the designation FL. This traffic officer arrives at the scene of an accident and prepares a report. *Springfield, Missouri, Police Archives*

"What do you want?" In this case, the user was the California Highway Patrol, reputed by Kawasaki sales managers to have the toughest standards of any agency in the world. Motor officers nationwide were subsequently asked for their suggestions. It was in this manner that Kawasaki challenged Harley's share of the police market by designing a police motorcycle according to the requirements of a motor officer.

While Kawasaki was staking a claim in police territory, Harley-Davidson was wondering about its future. Owned since 1969 by the conglomerate, AMF, Incorporated, Harley had lost

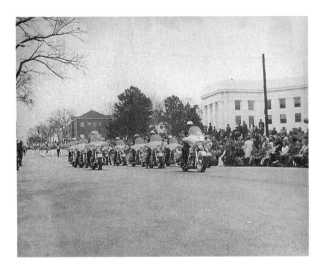

On January 18, 1971, Harley-Davidson motorcycles from the Mobile Police Department lead the inauguration parade for Governor Lurleen B. Wallace. *Mobile, Alabama, Police Archives*

sight of the importance of the police market and was not aggressively courting it. Harley had always dominated the market for larger motorcycles and was not prepared for the competition that came from the Japanese. In 1975, Harley-Davidson launched a long-range product strategy that eventually began to turn the company around. But it took years. In fact, ten years passed before police agencies testing new models noticed improvements in the Harley-Davidson police motorcycle.

Technological innovations that benefited police agencies included the introduction in 1971 of the FLH Electra-Glide, which was equipped with a 74ci, high-compression engine and ten-inch front disc brakes. In the mid-seventies, electronic sirens began to appear, although Harley-Davidson did not offer them as an option until about 1984. Harley stopped offering the mechanical siren in 1979. In 1978, the Electra-Glide featured a 1340cc, 80ci engine.

But in 1978, the Los Angeles Police Department stopped testing Harleys. The department felt that Kawasaki technology so conclusively outpaced Harley's engineering, that Harley stopped offering motorcycles for the annual evaluation. The LAPD wouldn't even test another Harley until around 1983.

Some departments began to structure their bid specifications to exclude the Harley-Davidson product. The bidding process is usually fairly simple. The department extends an invitation to dealers to bid. A detailed set of specifications is provided and the award goes to the lowest bidder. If specifications are written to describe a particular manufacturer (i.e., Kawasaki), other competitors (i.e., Harley) could be intentionally excluded from the bid on the technical grounds that their product did not meet the bid guidelines. This happened often, resulting in an ever-increasing number of Kawasaki purchases. But there was a loyalty factor, particularly in the East and Midwest, that enabled Harley-Davidson to endure through the hard times.

St. Louis, Missouri

On Saturday, July 26, 1958, the St. Louis Police Motorcycle Squad was quietly disbanded. Riders had been assigned to work a Missouri American Legion convention parade that day. After the parade, the motorcycles were never used again. By then, the squad was down to twelve motors, which were all sold the following year.

Suffolk County Police Highway Patrol officers line-up prior to a 1974 police funeral. The first motor in line has an electronic siren or PA speaker mounted above the headlight. *Suffolk County Police Museum*

Thirteen years later, on June 7, 1971, the department resumed use of motorcycles when twelve Harley-Davidsons were acquired through a U.S. Department of Transportation grant. Major Alexander Kaiser had been a member of the Traffic Division from 1939 to 1962, and was instrumental in getting the grant money to acquire the Harleys in 1971. Thirteen years of progress was evident.

In an article for the fall 1971 St. Louis Police Journal entitled, "Two-Wheelers Try it Again," Maj. Kaiser described some noteworthy improvements. The new Harleys were heavier and easier to ride; they also had wider tires. The motorcycles Kaiser remembered from the old days had unsprung rear ends and a sprung fork,

a particular disadvantage while riding along a cobblestone street. The new technology came with hydraulic rear shocks and hydraulic front forks. The old motors had kick starters, single exhausts, and a gearshift lever on the side of the gas tank. The new models had electric starters, double exhausts, and foot gearshifts.

The new motorcycle squad that resumed duty in 1971 received assignments based on computer mapping, including times and locations where patrol was needed most, supplementing the district's regular traffic enforcement efforts. The maneuverability of the motorcycle in heavy traffic made it highly useful. And unlike their colorful predecessors, the new motor officers were instructed never to participate in high speed chases. One thing remains the same, though, and that is a proud tradition and esprit de corps. A St. Louis citizen was quoted as saying: "The motorcycle policeman is the only man I ever saw who looks like he's strutting when he's sitting down."

Suffolk County Police Commissioner Eugene Kelly tries out the driver's seat of one of his department's sidecars. *Suffolk County Police Museum*

V-Twin Tales: Harleys on Patrol

Motor Officer Mike Bissett

Ofc. Mike Bissett has been riding motors with the Los Angeles Police Department since 1979. He first trained and rode for the department on a hand-me-down 1974 Harley-Davidson FLH. At the LAPD, there was an "old list" and a "new list" for fleet motorcycles. When a new guy came into motors, he received an older bike (i.e., hand-me-down) belonging to another officer, who then received a newer bike. The LAPD last bought Harleys for their fleet in 1974, with the last Harley being phased out by about 1987.

Ofc. Bissett recalled that in appearance and sound, the 1974 Harley-Davidson FLH was beautiful. When you polished the chrome and waxed the smart black-and-white paint scheme, it looked fabulous. He liked the heavy clutch and loved the low handlebars. You could customize the mirrors to suit your personal preference. Bissett liked to ride with the mirrors low, so he could look at them between his elbows and body. The leg room was good, enabling you to sit into the motorcycle. It had a big, broad seat that was generally very comfortable for slow riding. But the seat had a center post on a spring, which could jar the rider severely if he hit a dip in the road. The jolt could not be fully absorbed beyond the limits of the spring, so the rider's back took the remainder of the shock. The 1974 FLH looked good and it sounded good. But from there, it went downhill, especially when compared to the Kawasakis infiltrating the fleet. It is important to remember that police motor officers have a different set of expectations about the motorcycles they ride for police work. If their criticisms are harsh, it is because their riding is not necessarily pleasure cruising.

Ofc. Bissett recalled that the engine performance on the 1974 FLH was below average. At initial acceleration, it was slow and hesitant and at high speed it lacked sufficient power. For example, there's a stretch of freeway that goes over a long, steep hill from the Hollywood area where you need power to climb. Sometimes, especially if there was a hot, dry Santa Ana wind blowing off the desert, that old Harley could not get much above 40mph, and there were times when the rider was doubtful that the bike could even keep going. Because the motor was slow and hesitant from idle,

Harley riders developed the habit of revving the engine to prevent it from stalling. The motor officer always had this nagging fear that the motor would die just as he was pulling away. This was the last thing a police officer needed. Revving the motor became an involuntary reflex that many officers exhibit even today on their Kawasakis, which, in fact, never had such a problem with acceleration from idle.

Another disadvantage of the 1974 FLH was brake fade. The bikes were so heavy that the brakes just didn't last very long. Sometimes a driver would brake and never know what was going

In the summer of 1971, radio commentator Paul Harvey had a chance to visit with three motor officers from the Mobile Police Department. Mr. Harvey had a soft spot in his heart for law enforcement officers, since his father had been a policeman. Standing behind him are Officers Gill, Mair, and Parks. *Mobile, Alabama, Police Archives*

to happen. In a high-speed chase, the rider would often experience brake fade. At that time, LAPD officers were taught rear brake application only, because the department was going to Moto Guzzis, which had an integrated braking system. On the Moto Guzzi, when the foot brake was ap-

St. Louis Police motor officers stop for a quick photo in 1971. Fiberglass has now replaced the fabric or vinyl fairings. *St. Louis, Missouri, Police Archives*

fore, the department was afraid that if officers were taught to apply the front brake for Harley operation, they would continue to apply it when riding the Moto Guzzi, thereby risking a lock-up and possible crash. Riders were taught to apply the front brake only to straighten the bike if the Harley went sideways.

The suspension on the 1974 FLH was rated below average in the areas of bounce, turning, wobble, and drag on turns. Because of the low center of gravity, a driver could not lean very far into turns, so if the driver was chasing someone up a winding, mountain road it could be dangerous. And everything vibrated: handlebars, mirrors, windshield, footboards, gas tanks, lights, and safety bars. The mirrors became useless with the vibration. Ofc. Bissett had a new windshield break during a 95mph chase. He had three gas tanks on the right and two on the left replaced due to vibration. He had red lights crack and fall

plied, seventy percent of the braking went to the rear brake, and thirty percent went to the front, without actually applying the front brake. There-

BELOW
Officers Janice, Adams, Plehn, and Morgenstern of the Las Vegas Metropolitan Police Department's graveyard shift in April 1977. *Las Vegas, Nevada, Metro Police Archives*

A 1973 group shot of the Las Vegas Metropolitan Police Department motor unit. *Las Vegas, Nevada, Metro Police Archives*

off due to vibration, as did crash bars. The bike was often in the department garage.

Although it was mighty big, the police speedometer was located on the tank, so the officer had to look down to read it, which took his eyes off the road. The turn indicators were also poorly located on the tank, and had to be held down through the turn. This, however, was the technology of the day. There wasn't really anything better until the Japanese entered the market in the mid-seventies.

The Eighties

In the eighties, the Harley-Davidson police motorcycle, after a long struggle, regained it's strength in the police market.

Harley's market share continued to decline and AMF, Incorporated, was losing interest in its troublesome subsidiary. In early 1981, thirteen senior executives took over the company in a multi-million dollar leveraged buyout. An independent Harley-Davidson Motor Company was born in June 1981. In an effort to improve quality and productivity, the company involved employees in decisions and problem solving and improved manufacturing efficiency. They focused on the big bike niche and won protection against Japanese imports by virtue of substantial trade tariffs. A new, 1984 marketing strategy called "Super Ride" tried to convince customers that quality problems had been solved. But financial problems remained.

Harleys Under the Microscope

In the meantime, police agencies continued to evaluate the two major competitors. The 1983 Harley-Davidson 80ci, 1340cc (Shovelhead) model kept coming up short against the Kawasaki. Motor officers who tested it said it could not turn as tight, its average and peak speeds during a simulated pursuit were lower, its lap times were longer, its breaking distances were longer, its gas mileage was lower, it had an inferior horsepower-to-weight ratio, and darned if it didn't blow oil all over the test rider.

A summary statement was drafted in one department in which the following criticisms were made: the handlebars were uncomfortable due to the shape of the bars; the clutch engagement was stiff, fatiguing the rider's hands; the shift lever was poorly located,

By the mid-seventies, officers carried personal radios and wore helmets. Blue pursuit lights, effective for night visibility, shared equal space with red lights. This Wayne County (Michigan) Sheriff's motor unit still has the old siren system. *Michael Kan Collection*

1972 FLH, a survivor from the old days of the "suicide shifter" and foot-operated siren, although this unit is updated with a front disc brake. Officer Steve Clarence of the D.C. Metro Police has a mobile radio on his hip and a Motorola radio mounted on the motorcycle. On the tank, preceding the name "Harley-Davidson," are the letters, AMF. *Michael Kan Collection*

1979 FLH, part of the U.S. Park Police motor squad, which has among its duties that of dignitary escort for the President of the United States and for heads of state visiting Washington, D.C. *Michael Kan Collection*

requiring the officer to lift his foot from the floorboard to shift; the location of the rear brake control made the rider unable to ride with the right foot squarely on the footboard; the sidestand was not readily accessible in either the folded or extended positions; the windshield allowed wind to hit the rider in the face and chest from underneath the fairing as well as through the opening around the headlight where the fit was poor; stability was found to be unacceptable; engine vibration was excessive, whether at idle or while moving; turning was unsatisfactory, since the frame and footboard dragged at a forty-five degree lean; the top speed of 92mph was unsatisfactory; and the seat was uncomfortable after two hours of riding. The department felt that this particular motorcycle did not meet the established specifications covering performance, hand and foot controls, comfort, speed, engine performance, noise, and vibration. It was recommended that the 1983 Harley-Davidson police motorcycle not be approved for traffic enforcement applications for that particular department for the coming year.

By the early eighties, the competition eroded Harley-Davidson's share of the police market by more than twenty-five percent. The importance of the police market could not be underestimated. Motorcycle manufacturers agree that sales to police agencies stimulate overall sales to their civilian consumers. A motor officer is a living advertisement for the product. Even though the police market represented only about ten percent of Harley's total sales in 1983, the importance of the market could not be ignored. But money problems at the corporate level persisted.

By 1984, Citicorp was no longer interested in being Harley's corporate lender and was no longer willing to extend over advances beyond a negotiated six-month time frame. As attorneys worked on a bankruptcy plan, executives searched for another corporate lender. Finally, in December 1985, a deal was struck with Heller Financial Corporation, whose number two executive happened to be a Harley buff. It's astounding to realize that during these incredibly difficult years, a new engine was on the drawing board.

In 1984, after seven years of development, the 1340cc V-twin Evolution™ engine was introduced. A belt final drive system with a five-speed transmission and a rubber-mounted engine were just a few of the improvements. Many believe that this engine saved the company. There is no doubt that it invigorated the police motorcycle market and signaled Harley-Davidson's desire to regain police customers.

Indeed, the 1985 police model had greatly improved, but controversy continued to brew within police departments as to which machine was truly superior, the Harley or the Kawasaki. Performance, reliability, comfort, and safety were issues hotly debated as agencies took

Officer Rich Cademartori sits proudly on his black-and-white 1979 FLH. The Oakland Police Department has been a longtime customer of Harley-Davidson. An electronic siren speaker is mounted on the rear safety guard. *Michael Kan Collection*

bids each year. When they took a look at the 1985 model, the departments that had rated the 1983 Harley police motorcycle unfit for traffic patrol discovered a dramatic improvement.

Partially hidden on the opposite side of this 1972 FL is a sidecar. This is one of the last hand-shift models. The front wheel brake caliper has an aluminum cover. *Michael Kan Collection*

This mid-seventies FL is well equipped for visibility with front and rear rotating beacons and front and rear red pursuit lights. The Henrico County (Virginia) Police Logo graces the side of the tank. The officer is wearing a three-quarter helmet with boom microphone. *Michael Kan Collection*

The 1985 FXRP (Pursuit Glide) was evaluated by members of one department in the following areas: engine performance, clutch, brakes, suspension, seat, vibration, transmission,

This 1972 FL is painted white and "Pepsi" blue, the colors of all NYPD marked vehicles. *Michael Kan Collection*

balance and stability, handlebars, controls, instruments, and miscellaneous (crash bars, sidestand, windshield, fairing, and saddlebags). In general, the problem areas were few but consistent among motor officers filling out the evaluation sheets. Most had difficulty starting the engine, most agreed that vibration was highest at idle, downshifting was hard or rough, seat comfort needed improvement, the sidestand was still troublesome, and the fairing was still letting too much wind through. But in all other areas, the performance of this model was good.

What follows is a series of quotes from motor officers who rode the new 1985 FXRP (Pursuit Glide) model for a two-week period on regular patrol. Keep in mind that the fleet contained some Kawasakis to which the officers were often assigned. The quotes were taken directly from the comment section of standardized evaluation sheets:

"This motorcycle is a definite improvement over the old Harley-Davidson. Its most commendable feature is the smooth ride at cruising speeds…[however] at the end of a working shift, I experienced much more body fatigue with this motorcycle than normal."

"Because of the seat design (flat), any hard acceleration or hard braking leaves the rider sliding forward and back. Overall, I feel this is a good motorcycle and it excels in the road department…. On a daily basis, in a stop-and-go situation, I found it to be tiring. At the end of the day, I was ready to get off."

"The bike is a pleasure to ride. It is smoother than the Kawasaki and has excellent handling capabilities…. The engine has the tendency to not kick over and start…. Another poor feature of this model is the hand switches or buttons for the turn signals…you have to keep the button depressed in order to make the turn signal function. This is somewhat of a hindrance when the operator is attempting to brake, shift gears, and turn a corner at the same time…. I was quite pleased with the bike, but would be unwilling to make the change until Harley decides to change the aforementioned problems."

"The rear brakes were in a class all their own…fourth class. To get the rear brake required bending the right leg in and around the air-cleaner, then onto the pedal. The pedal had a mushy feel and gave no warning towards rear wheel lockup…. The sidestand was difficult to reach, and then once obtained, had to be gently lowered or it would bounce back. One would not exit the motor in a hurry if you expected it to be in an upright position upon your return.... The handlebar switches were a nightmare. The high/low beam switch is next to the siren wail switch. To use the high/low switch, it was necessary to reach across the siren switch, then attempt to activate it without turning the siren on. On the opposite side, the engine start and engine kill switches are also identical. It was very easy to accidentally press the start button instead of the kill button. The engine let you know immediately, sounding something like a hundred roofing nails in a garbage disposal.... Overall, the Harley-Davidson is an adequate motorcycle, but still needs improvement."

"The first thing I noticed was that the motorcycle was a good looking bike; not big and bulky looking as in the past. The engine performance was good, but starting was very slow.... The controls are still the old style Harley. Why should a rider have to hold a finger on the turn signal continuously to keep it on? Why does the key have to be on the gas tank? Overall, the Harley is a good motorcycle for simple road driving. But for constant stop-go, start-stop, and fast driving, it's still the old Harley. If [designers] would simply use the modern technology available to make what would be simple changes, it would be a useful work tool. But, in its present condition, it's too cumbersome."

"Harley-Davidson should be congratulated on the new [1985] FXRP. It is a giant improvement over the old Harley. At no time during the testing did I find anything that would make the FXRP unacceptable as a police motorcycle, with the exception of the acceleration phase. However, it, again, in my opinion, does not totally compare with the Kawasaki."

Feedback like this, however, would serve to keep the pressure on Harley-Davidson to continue to improve police bikes with each new model year. By the nineties, most of the bugs were gone, and Kawasaki riders were hard-pressed to find significant objections to the new Harley-Davidson police models.

The face-off between Harley-Davidson and Kawasaki took place in California. The numbers at stake were great, with the California Highway Patrol and the Los Angeles Police Department representing the biggest single purchaser of motorcycles in the United States. In addition, a political debate was raging concerning the "buy American" issue. In April 1983, new tariffs were imposed on large-displacement motor-

While not offered by Harley-Davidson as a police motorcycle in 1979, the City of Torrance, California, adapted this 1000cc Sportster to its motor needs. *Michael Kan Collection*

cycles. This twenty percent tariff effectively increased the price of the foreign motorcycles, making the Harleys less costly by comparison.

In 1984, the California Highway Patrol announced its purchase of 183 Harley-Davidson police motorcycles (1985 FXRPs). The CHP had not even tested a Harley since the late seventies,

This detail photo of a mid-eighties FXRP shows the pride motor officers have in their motorcycles and in their personal appearance. The high boots are spit-shined to a military gloss. Even hard-to-reach places on this Harley are spotless. The electronic siren produces a combination of yelps and wails. *Michael Kan Collection*

This mid-eighties FXRP patrolled California freeways along with members of the Kawasaki breed. Whenever the television series "CHiPs" is mentioned in conversation, Harley enthusiasts claim that if actor Erik Estrada had been riding a Harley instead of a Kawasaki, he'd still be on TV today. *Michael Kan Collection*

so gaining the CHP back as a customer was very important to Harley-Davidson. It was a positive image that helped them recover their sales in the state of California, and was part of the recovery process. To celebrate, Harley-Davidson created a print ad campaign featuring a motor officer astride the new 1985 FXRP. The headline reads: "We just got picked up in California." The Los Angeles Police Department, on the other hand, did not return to the Harley-Davidson police motorcycle. It phased out the last Harley in the fleet in around 1987. Nevertheless, beginning with the introduction of this new model, Harley-Davidson began picking up new police customers at a rate of about fifty to seventy-five each year. The Kawasaki-Harley debate became an East versus West phenomenon, with police agencies in the East remaining loyal to Harley and less open to Kawasaki.

The two rocker shafts in each cylinder head identify this Harley as being powered by the Shovelhead motor. This Farmington Hills (Michigan) Police motorcycle is finished in blue and white. *Michael Kan Collection*

Officer Skip Gage of the Detroit (Michigan) Police Department looks like he enjoys riding his 1980 FLH. *Michael Kan Collection*

One of the ten big Harley-Davidson police motorcycles owned by the city of Chicago. The only duty of these motors is VIP motorcade escort. This 1985 FLHTP has a little over 9,000 miles on the odometer. The large, chrome air-cleaner is affectionately called a "ham can."

RIGHT
Early eighties Shovelhead-powered Harley of the U.S. Park Police, Washington D.C. *Michael Kan Collection*

Chicago's Harleys are white with a blue star on the tank and fairing.

RIGHT
The rear rack is empty, since the motorcycles used by the city of Chicago have no radios installed; instead, officers carry personal radios.

Officer James Rapata has been assigned to the motorcade unit for over ten years, and says that motorcade duty is a matter of "hurry up and wait." The most memorable escort was when former Soviet leader Mikhail Gorbachev stopped by the Hard Rock Cafe for a beer on the way to O'Hare Airport.

NEXT PAGE
The right front safety guard mounts the speaker for the siren/PA. The electronic control for the siren is mounted on the left rear of the safety guard.

CHAPTER 9

The Nineties: Performance Back on Patrol

The Harley-Davidson Motor Company continued to improve the police model. They gained recognition in corporate circles for improving quality and saving a company that was on the brink of bankruptcy. What better place to go for hands-on information about these new models than to the people who ride them. The two police motorcycles offered by Harley-Davidson through 1994 were the Electra-Glide (FLHTP) and the Pursuit Glide (FXRP).

Las Vegas Metropolitan Police
In early 1990, the Las Vegas Metropolitan Police Department embarked on its annual evaluation of police motorcycles for the coming year. Their story is no different than that found within many police departments throughout the nation at that time. Although Harley-Davidson Motor Company, Incorporated, had made consistent improvements in their police product since 1985, the preference for the Kawasaki was still entrenched in the hearts of many people, particularly those in the West. Unlike the dare-devils of the twenties and thirties who just jumped on the nearest thing with a motor and careened down a gravel road holding on to their soft caps, today's officers are educated, well-trained professionals who demand that they sit on the best equipment available on the market. The product must stand on its own. It must measure up to a set of strict requirements laid out by members of law enforcement for whom the machine was their "office." The comparison had to be scientific, fair, and relevant to daily use on the job.

Michigan State Trooper Trevor Radke on his 1994 FLHTP. The Michigan State Police reintroduced motorcycles as freeway patrol vehicles in 1994, after an absence of fifty years. The motorcycle of choice? A Harley-Davidson, of course. *Michael Kan Collection*

No one could argue with the number of improvements that had been made on the police Harley since 1985. The 1991 model had a new starter, carburetor, clutch, exhaust system,

Officers Paul Lauer (left) and David Ramsey pose by their 1994 FLHTP Harleys. Large, white fairings provide an increased degree of visibility for motorists. *St. Louis, Missouri, Police Archives*

speedometer, tachometer, fuel gauge, front forks, seat, alternator, intake manifolds, and turn signals. It had a thicker, breakaway windshield and a fiberglass fairing. The 1991 model had over three hundred new parts, including a completely new frame and engine mounting system. Although many motor officers still preferred Kawasakis, results of testing indicated a vast improvement over previous years (pre-1985) in which the Harley was scorned by some as unacceptable for police work.

In order to illustrate these improvements, we must rely on the feedback from officers who tested this model. We are grateful to the Las Vegas Metropolitan Police Department for sharing some of their positive impressions of the 1991 model. Although skepticism among some officers persisted, Harley-Davidson had demonstrated its commitment to making a better product.

Two officers were assigned to operate one Kawasaki and one Harley (1991 FXRP Pursuit

Glide) on the department's training courses for one day. They covered the same skill activities that all members of the traffic section are required to complete from time to time. Both motorcycles passed the test. The performance of the motorcycles was closely matched. Differences were in the areas of braking, where Harley exhibited greater braking ability (i.e., in a shorter distance), while the Kawasaki had a faster time around the obstacle course.

Six other officers were assigned to operate the machines in the real world for a period of two weeks. Although the Kawasaki scored higher among the officers, the Harley was not far behind, and both motorcycles were evaluated to be totally acceptable and capable for police work.

Sgt. Tom Plehn of the Las Vegas Metropolitan Police Department wrote a narrative summary about the changes to this model over previous years in a campaign to include Harleys in dual-source bidding. Many of the improvements were in direct response to complaints lodged earlier about the perceived flaws in the Harley police model. We borrow freely from Sgt. Plehn's narrative to illustrate these improvements.

On Ezzerd Charles Drive, across from police headquarters in Cincinnati, stands a memorial dedicated to the officers who have lost their lives in the line of duty. Etched onto the face of the marble monument is the likeness of Cincinnati Motor Officer Robert Leigh astride a 1939 Harley-Davidson police motorcycle. He was killed on April 27, 1940. Parked in front of the memorial is a 1993 FLHTP. Note the large, side facing strobe on the rear compartment.
Cincinnati, Ohio, Police Archives

Riding and Handling: The FXRP passes over roadway bumps and irregularities very smoothly. The suspension system is soft and compliant. Straight line and high speed cornering stability are excellent. The Harley-Davidson possesses a very neutral steering response. After the turn has been established, the FXRP will continue the turning rate as selected without the need for constant steering adjustments by the rider. The bike was almost totally unaffected by wind gusts.

Performance: The Harley-Davidson will out-accelerate its competitor in a throttle roll-on from about 50 to 60mph in fifth gear. This is a handy feature for changing lanes through holes in traffic. The abundance of low rpm torque al-

lows operation with a minimum of downshifting. A common problem among officers new to or not properly trained on Harleys is excessive up and down shifting. (Interestingly, it was noted that technological improvements in both machines far exceed the riding capabilities of most riders).

Vibration: With the engine mounted in rubber mounts, engine vibration is felt only at idle, and fades completely by 1500rpm. The Harley-Davidson's engine vibration is very sensitive to idle adjustment. Careful adjustment of idle speed will reduce vibration at these low rpm's significantly. The faster the Harley is ridden, the smoother it becomes.

Brakes: Both front and rear brakes on the Harley-Davidson are smooth action with a progressive feel. The motorcycles come from the factory with DOT-5 silicone brake fluid, giving an enhanced margin of safety, as DOT-5 will not boil.

Fairings: The still-air pocket of the Harley-Davidson fairing covers the rider from just above the boot tops to the top of the head. There is very little collapsing of the air pocket onto the rider. As an option, fairing-lowers can be purchased, which when attached to the bottom of the fair-

Chula Vista (California) Police Motor Officers Eric Tarr (left) and Kelly Harris enter one of Southern California's freeways on their FXRPs.

ing, cover the entire leg and foot area. There is also improved storage capacity in the fairing.

Seat: The seat can be adjusted from front to back, up or down, forward or back, or according to different sizes and weights of riders. The extra spring action of these seats smoothes the ride while operating over rough city streets.

Handlebars and Controls: The handlebars on the Harley are angled so the operator can reach out and grip them without angling the wrists at all. This allows for more comfort and control. The clutch lever can also be rotated on the handlebar to allow it to be adjusted for different grip sizes. Switches are much larger and easier to use, especially with heavy gloves. There is also a thumb-wheel on the right handlebar to cancel out the return spring on the throttle.

Radio Mounting: The radio is secured to a bracket on the gas tank, allowing the eight-pound weight to be carried by the frame instead of the steering area. An additional benefit of a tank-mounted radio is that the microphone can be operated with either hand.

Saddlebags: Made from a tough, flexible plastic, they can be latched with one movement.

Floorboards: The floorboards are mounted closer together, due to the reduced width of the engine, thus making for a more comfortable riding position.

Transmission: The Harley can be shifted into neutral while the bike is still moving, allowing an officer to have a free hand with which to make radio contact with dispatch, while attempting to stop the vehicle.

Belt-Driven System: Equipped with a Kevlar™-reinforced belt as its final drive, the operation is very quiet. As a safety feature, it's unlikely that a belt would break and cause a rear

The saddlebags on police motors are filled with goodies, including a ticket book and a pair of gloves. The saddlebag on the left side has space for a jacket.

wheel to lock up as a result of it wrapping around the rear sprocket.

Sidestand: The Harley-Davidson sidestand is designed to retract automatically upon contact with the roadway in the event the rider attempts to drive off with the sidestand in the down position.

Carburetor: Several complaints of rough idling, coughing, or sputtering through the carburetor were reported with the 1985 through 1988 police models. Harley-Davidson installed a completely new carburetor on all 1990 motorcycles. Carburetor size was increased, making it a constant velocity type with an accelerator pump.

Starters: Beginning in 1989, an improved starter was provided on police models. This new starter eliminates the lag caused in turning over the engine.

Alternators: The 1985 Harley suffered from battery problems caused by the low amperage output of the alternator system. This problem was corrected in 1989 with the installation of a 30amp alternator.

Turn signals: With the 1991 model, all police Harleys were fitted with self-canceling turn signals. In addition, its four-way flasher system provides better visibility at night, in a Code-3 situation, or simply when making a routine traffic stop. Finally, Harleys can be ordered with what are called CHP sidelights for additional rear lighting protection.

Exhaust Design: The exhaust system on the Harley-Davidson does not present a hazard to the properly dressed operator. The exhaust pipe is routed in an area that provides no contact with the rider. Also, all exposed surfaces of the pipes are covered with a shield that reduces the temperature of exposed sections of the exhaust system. The design also keeps the exhaust pipes from being damaged while riding over medians and curbs, because the frame of the motorcycle is the motorcycle's lowest point. Harley-Davidson

The left-hand grip on this 1990 FXRP has controls for lights, siren, turn signals, and horn. The small micro switch is for the radio. The officer depresses the switch to talk.

145

Neatly tucked into the left side of the fairing just below the voltmeter is the motor officer's companion—the ticket book.

RIGHT
A rear view of this FXRP reveals a very compact package. The radar gun's coiled power cord can be seen to the right of the right saddlebag. The microphone on the right-hand side of the fairing is for the PA system.

has a different exhaust system available at no additional cost, if it is specified on the bid instructions. It's called the High Performance Exhaust System, and it increases the motorcycle's power by two to three horsepower and lessens the noise level. The two small mufflers on the right side are replaced with two large mufflers, one located on each side of the rear wheel.

The Las Vegas Metropolitan Police Department purchased two additional motorcycles for its fleet, one 1990 Kawasaki and one 1991 Harley-Davidson FXRP.

Las Vegas Metropolitan Police: 1993–A Longer Look
Once again, the department embarked on an evaluation of the 1993 Harley-Davidson FLHTP Electra-Glide Police Motorcycle. This model was on loan to the department for a period of ninety days. During that time, it was ridden over 6,000 miles over a two-week period by fifteen different motor officers, all of whom then com-

pleted an eleven-page evaluation sheet. On a scale of zero to ten, this model averaged an eight, with individual scores ranging from a low of 4.9 to a high of 9.8.

To discuss the features and improvements of this model, we again borrow freely from Sgt. Plehn's summary of these evaluations. The following items were given special consideration: fairing; fuel system; suspension; frame; floorboards; saddlebags and radio box; switches, controls, and instruments; ignition switch; engine and transmission; electrical system; and motorcycle stands.

Fairing: The fairing is mounted directly onto the fork. This allows it to be positioned closer to the rider, affording much better wind protection for not only the torso and head area, but for the arms and especially the hands. In addition to increasing officer comfort, it has three areas that improve officer safety. The fairing allows the radio and speaker to be mounted directly into the fairing. This eliminates the need for a large number of heavy, metal brackets to be bolted onto the handlebars or the gas tank. This speaker and radio head combination presented considerable hazard to the officer's groin area in the event of an accident. The new Harley removes these obstructions. The fairing of the new Harley allows the light beam from the headlight to be directed by the rider by moving the handlebars. This allows the rider to avoid hazards at lower speeds at night. All instrumentation in the fairing is visible and readable. The speedometer and other instruments are located high in the fairing and are placed at an angle that allows excellent viewing.

Fuel system: The new Harley allows for a capacity of 5.2 gallons. This extra fuel increases the range by about forty miles. The tank is designed to be refueled by the vapor recovery nozzle without unnecessary manipulation by the operator. This tank is supplied with a lock and covered to prevent fuel tampering.

Suspension: The front fork includes an adjustable air suspension system that can be pressurized to adjust the spring rate for various

Who says cops don't have a sense of humor!

load conditions. It also incorporates a unique anti-dive system that helps to reduce forward weight transfer under heavy braking. The rear suspension uses adjustable air shocks in place of the manual spring pre-loads. These shocks prevent the system from bottoming out while under severe compression. These shock absorbers working in conjunction with the spring mounted seat help to prevent back injuries.

Frame: The Electra-Glide utilizes a frame with several important changes over our current model. The Electra-Glide uses a system with the fork tubes mounted behind the steering pivot point. This allows the frame of the motorcycle to pull, not push, the front wheel assembly when in operation. This creates a balanced steering system that allows the motorcycle to be completely stable at high speeds, but still respond with quick light steering at slow speeds. Many of the test riders were impressed by the easy handling of this large and impressive motorcycle, stating that it rode and handled like a much smaller machine.

The speedometer on this FXRP is calibrated for accuracy.

These traits are directly linked to the unique and innovative front frame assembly.

Floorboards: The new frame makes provisions for an improved mounting of hinged floorboards that can be adjusted to accommodate the rider's preference.

Today's motorcycles are wired at the factory so the headlight remains on at all times. Police agencies, however, have the option to turn it off as needed for certain types of patrol work. When riding in pairs, the officer on the left is usually the lead pilot.

Saddlebags and Radio Box: The longer length of the frame allows the large radio boxes to be mounted far enough to the rear to prevent contact by the rider's belt and equipment. All electrical equipment, siren amplifier, and strobe can be mounted into this large, radio box, leaving the saddlebags unobstructed and clear for the officer's use. The fiberglass saddlebags have almost twice the capacity of our old models. The unique latching system is easy to use and can be operated with one hand while sitting on the motorcycle. The locking device is secured with the ignition key.

Switches, Controls, and Instruments: The new Electra-Glide possesses the best instrument package of any police motorcycle. Both speedometer and tachometer are mounted in the fairing area, not on the handlebars. Other instruments mounted in this cluster include a clock, voltmeter, fuel gauge, oil pressure, neutral, turn signal, and high beam and pursuit lights. The following switches are mounted on the handlebars: headlight, high/low beam, self-canceling turn signals, flashers, ignition kill switch, starter, and pursuit and siren switches. The throttle is equipped with a spring tension adjusting device that allows the operator to dial out the throttle return spring, if desired. Both the clutch and brake leverage have been redesigned for comfort and ease of operation.

Ignition Switch: The Electra-Glide possesses an unusual ignition switch that is integrated with a fork lock that automatically allows the

Two FXRPs from the Chula Vista (California) Police Department. In the foreground is a 1990 model, and in the background is a 1991.

fork to be locked in the full, left-turn position. The switch also allows the machine to be operated without the key remaining in the ignition switch.

Engine and Transmission: Several important changes have been made in these areas. The oil tank has been relocated from under the seat to the bottom of the transmission. You can check the oil without removing the seat. In 1991, the clutch was completely redesigned and now rides on a splined shaft, which prevents any torque transfer to the locking nut. The engine breathing system has been re-engineered and no longer causes loss of oil through the air-cleaner. The location of the shift lever is no longer directed through the primary case, thus preventing oil loss from the primary chain case. The exhaust system is totally redesigned with the two large mufflers replacing the two smaller duals on our current Harley-Davidson models, making it one of the quietest motorcycles we operate.

Electrical System: The new model comes with a much larger battery. At no time during this evaluation did a motorcycle require a jump start or push due to a failure to start, even during many long hours of radar operation on the swing and graveyard shifts, when all of the lights are in constant use and the electrical system is placed under its heaviest demand.

Motorcycle Stands: The sidestand has been relocated to a position nearer to the front of the frame to aid in operation. The old location required the officer to reach to the rear with his leg to deploy the stand. It's now easy to locate the stand just to the rear of the left floorboard. The sidestand is not equipped with an electronic kill switch; instead, it retracts by itself if the rider attempts to drive the motorcycle with the sidestand in the down position. The center stand on the Electra-Glide supports the machine in an upright position with both wheels firmly in contact with the ground. An officer can sit in an upright position with feet on the floorboards without teetering. This position is a very comfortable one for working radar. The officer needs only to place the machine in gear and ride off the center stand.

In the comment section of the written evaluations, some of the evaluating officers wrote about a few drawbacks they found with the 1993 FLHTP. One officer had trouble with the kickstand and felt that the acceleration was a little slow. Another thought he would like a slightly higher windshield and found shifting uncomfortable. One officer felt a little high in the saddle, but thought the feeling might go away as he got used to the bike. He also mentioned that this model would be better out on the open highway, as opposed to working the city streets. Another suggested longer arms on the mirrors and a longer rear shift lever. One officer recommended a hi-low switch for the radio. Another thought the front pursuit light should be of the strobe variety and felt the field of vision in the mirrors was reduced somewhat. Finally, one officer stated that, although he preferred the FLHTP over the FXRP, he did not like the handling of the FLH on the city streets.

The following statements were made by the same officers in their written evaluations of the 1993 Harley-Davidson FLHTP:

"I thoroughly enjoyed the time spent riding the H-D FLHTP test bike. It was the most comfortable motorcycle I have ever ridden. All in all, it proved to be a reliable, duty-worthy motorcycle. I'd be proud to ride one."

All vehicles of the Michigan State Police are finished in a unique and traditional shade of blue. The MSP shield and gold lightning bolt appear on the tank. *Michigan State Police Archives*

LEFT
Sgt. Tom Plehn of the Las Vegas Metro Police on his FXRP. The Nevada desert gets cold in the winter and Sgt. Plehn is dressed for the season wearing a gold turtleneck sweater and a traditional leather jacket. The nineties leg shield design is made of fiberglass. *Las Vegas, Nevada, Metro Police Archives*

"Very comfortable and smooth at highway speeds. The best police model Harley-Davidson I've ridden, in both appearance and performance."

"A smooth and quiet performing machine. Excellent hand controls. Excellent public relations tool. Excellent resale value!"

"The most noticeable difference was the acceleration being a lot smoother (without the hitch in the carburetor), compared to the old H-D. The balance and turning was also noticeably improved. All in all, I thought the motorcycle was very good and would volunteer to ride one."

"After logging approximately 140 hours on the FLH, I found it to be a solid platform for police work. The biggest difference on the FLH was the public opinion, which was nothing less than incredible. Performance-wise, the FLH was more than adequate. Acceleration was good, starting was fast. The suspension was comfortable and easily adjustable for every rider's needs and size. The suspension never bottomed out or gave a harsh ride and made the FLH sure-footed in the corners at both high and low speeds on varied terrain. The best improvement in the engine and transmission was that it shifted smooth and positive with no missed shifts."

" A very strong and comfortable motor. The ride-off center stand and large saddlebags are a bonus. The rider position for my large frame is excellent because of the forward mounted floorboards. I was very comfortable all shift. Not as quick as the Kawi, but I caught all my speeders easily and safely. I would ride this motorcycle if they were purchased."

"This motorcycle in my opinion is the perfect police motorcycle. Its handling is outstanding along with all aspects of this vehicle."

"Having never ridden a Harley in my eleven years in traffic, I was surprised by its comfort, acceleration, and top end. One can get used to riding anything, especially if the alternative is four wheels."

"Overall, I was very surprised and pleased with this bike. The riding position and stability, especially in the wind, were excellent. Comfort was very good. This is an excellent cruising bike."

These positive comments are cited here not to serve as an advertisement for Harley-Davidson Motor Company, but to demonstrate how much the 1993 FLHTP had improved over previous model years. Even though some officers would still prefer to ride Kawasakis if given a choice, personal preference did not prevent them from recognizing the improvements in the new model and rating it an average of eight on a scale of zero to ten. In his summary, Sgt. Plehn stated that he believed "it is completely valid to find both brands of motorcycles acceptable for our use, but at the same time still prefer to ride one and not the other."

And, finally, a word about maintenance. The Las Vegas Metropolitan Police Department found that maintenance costs and downtime have improved with the 1991 model year and compare well with the Kawasaki. The department compared the maintenance records of

Sgt. Tracy McDonald of the Las Vegas Metro Police on an FLHTP. The boom microphone allows radio broadcasts and communication without removing hands from the controls. *Las Vegas, Nevada, Metro Police Archives*

In October 1994, members of the Las Vegas Metro Police motor unit gather at the Luxor Hotel for a photo op. *Las Vegas, Nevada, Metro Police Archives*

Several motorcycles patrol the Dallas/Ft. Worth International Airport. This type of patrol vehicle is well suited to a large airport with its vast parking lots and congested streets. This officer is riding an FXRP. *Michael Kan Collection*

their two newest motorcycles, a 1990 Kawasaki and a 1991 Harley FXRP. At 22,000 miles of similar operation, both had been in the shop about twenty-three times, and the difference in cost per mile was only three cents, with the Harley costing less to operate. Sgt. Plehn stated that "the Harley-Davidson Company has fixed what used to break on their motorcycles and, as has been shown by the description of the new 1993 Electra-Glide, they have continued to improve from 1991 to date [August 1993]."

Michigan State Police: Harley Returns

During the winter of 1941–42, the motorcycle unit of the Michigan State Police was disbanded. All motorcycles were brought into police headquarters and sold. Another fifty years passed before Harley-Davidson motorcycles rode on patrol on behalf of the Michigan State Police.

In the summer of 1993, the Michigan State Police conducted a three-month pilot program to determine the effectiveness of motorcycle patrols on the sixty-seven miles of freeways in the City of Detroit. Police cars had patrolled this freeway system since 1976. The need for better mobility in reaching the scene of accidents and in navigating to and through areas of major traffic congestion prompted the idea to test motorcycles.

The University of Michigan Traffic Research Institute conducted the study in which eleven motor officers took part riding Harley-Davidson FLHTPs and FXRPs. The results of the study showed that motorcycle officers spent more time on patrol, accumulated more miles, gave out more speeding citations, investigated more traffic accidents, and issued more seat belt violations per hour than patrol officers in cars. Because of their mobility in and around heavy traffic, motorcycles averaged twenty-four miles per patrol hour compared to fifteen miles for patrol cars. Finally, speeding citations were issued from motorcycles at a rate of 2.4 per hour, compared with 0.80 per hour from patrol cars.

An unexpected benefit of a motorcycle patrol was the positive response from the public. Some officers said they had fewer arguments with violators over citations. Most citizens were openly curious about the motorcycles and the research project. Because of the mobility and effectiveness of the motorcycles, and due to the positive response from the public and from within the department, motorcycles returned on a permanent basis as of June 1, 1994. After nearly fifty years, Michigan State Police Troopers were back on Harleys patrolling Detroit freeways. Of course, all are painted the traditional blue of the MSP.

Cincinnati Police Department

In June 1993, after much footwork and phone calls to other police agencies, the Cincinnati Police Department took delivery of two new Harley-Davidson FLHTP motorcycles. Fortunately for Cincinnati, they spared themselves the roller coaster ride of the seventies and eighties with respect to the competition between Harley and Kawasaki, although they may have heard plenty from other police agencies. Cincinnati is using two-wheel Harleys for the first time since 1961! The motorcycles are assigned to District One of the Cincinnati Police Division, which covers the central business district and the central river front areas. Motor officers do the same type of work as patrol officers, with the exception of prisoner transportation. The department is in the process of purchasing two additional Harley model FLHTPs. By the end of 1996, there could be as many as seven Harley-Davidson motorcycles patrolling the streets of Cincinnati.

Kansas City Police Department

In 1991, the motorcycle unit for the Kansas City Police Department was back.

The stylish tank logo designed for the Salt Lake City Motor Squad by one of its motor officers. Just below and to the right is the fuel valve. Fun-loving motor officers have been known to shut that valve off as soon as an unsuspecting buddy was looking the other way. This was even funnier, of course, in the days of kick starters.

Phased out in 1974, it had been seventeen years since motors patrolled the city streets. A dramatic increase in the number of traffic fatalities was the reason for bringing back the motor unit. The city hoped that the high visibility created by officers riding motorcycles would reduce the number of speed-related traffic fatalities.

Riding 1991 Harley-Davidson FXRPs, the five-person unit contributed to a reduction in the number of fatalities. In 1993, a grant from the Department of Transportation enabled the department to purchase seven additional Harleys. "Excessive speed is the number one cause for traffic accidents," said Captain George Trzok said in an article appearing in the Kansas City Kansan newspaper. "The visibility of our motorcycle unit throughout the community reminds our citizens how important it is to slow down and drive safely."

Officer Michael Chard of the Salt Lake City Police Department at speed on his FXRP.

Metro Transit Police, Washington, D.C.
In 1990, the Metro Transit Police proposed adding a Police Motorcycle unit to help pa-

When asked what other job he would choose if he could have any job in the world other than that of a motor officer riding a Harley, Ofc. Chard replied with a grin, "F-16 pilot."

trol the vast network of metro stations, trains and buses, and the properties incidental to transit operations (parking lots, garages, and track) under the jurisdiction of the Washington Metropolitan

High-speed stability!

Area Transit Authority. The department is unique in that it is a Transit Police Department and the only tri-state (Virginia, Maryland, and the District of Columbia) department in the country.

Above ground and underground parking facilities had a projected capacity of over 38,000 vehicles. It was in these parking areas where thirty-five percent of the 1,000 reported crimes took place in 1989. Reported crimes included auto theft, destruction of property, theft, robberies, and assaults. Sixty-five percent of the reported

crimes took place in the stations and trains serving bus and rail passengers and commuters. The city felt that a very visible and mobile motor unit would deter crime and stop more crimes in progress in these areas.

Although methods of policing these areas included foot and vehicle patrol, it was felt that the presence of motorcycles would improve overall effectiveness. The justification for the use of motorcycles included: improved response time and better mobility, increased officer safety, higher level of presence, enhanced coverage, crime prevention and crime patrol, more efficient traffic control, coverage due to special events, public relations, and officer morale.

The 1992 Harley-Davidson FLHTP was chosen for this assignment, meeting the requirements for dependability, serviceability, comfort, safety, unit function, resale value, and maintenance. Today, two FLHTPs form this small but mighty unit. The Washington Metropolitan Area Transit Authority now boasts one of the lowest crime rates of all transit systems.

V-Twin Tales: Harleys on Patrol

Motor Officer George L. Rosemeyer

Officer George L. Rosemeyer joined the Pittsburgh (Pennsylvania) Police Department in 1965, but didn't go into motors until 1980, where he remained until his retirement in November 1993. His first solo motorcycle was a 1976 Harley-Davidson. They rode the big 1979 Harleys for a number of years until 1987, when the department purchased the smaller 1987 FXRP. The last motor Rosemeyer rode for the department was a 1990 FXRP with sidecar. The sidecar is removed in April and installed in November. It's important to remember what month you're in when this change is made!

When November arrives, the city calls all the bikes in and sidecars are installed; officers ride with the sidecars all winter. The first week in April, the bikes are all called back in and the sidecars are removed. One spring day, the garage mechanics had just removed the sidecar from Ofc. Rosemeyer's motor. He drove out of the city garage and pulled over to the city pumps, which were just two buildings away. He got off the motorcycle, reached for the pump, and watched the bike fall over. Not remembering that the sidecar had just been removed, he hadn't put the kickstand down. There happened to be four police cars getting gas at the pumps, and the other officers thought this was just about the funniest thing they had ever seen.

People are amazed that Pittsburgh motor officers ride during the winter, even in snowy conditions. The only reason for having the sidecar is to keep the motorcycle upright. Without it, you'd be down a lot in that weather. Maneuvering the sidecar in the snow is a whole new way of riding. Officers can go pretty well in the snow with the sidecar, since the traction is good. But turning can be a problem. Although there is a regular tire on the sidecar, it has no traction for turning. The only wheel having traction is the front wheel. And even this wheel has only about two inches of rubber on the road. There were times when Ofc. Rosemeyer motored down the street, put the turn signal on to make a right-hand turn, and felt the bike continue to go straight, having insufficient traction to make the turn. So he would just go down to the next street and make a right turn as if he had planned it that way.

To keep warm while on patrol in the snow, officers are issued an orange rain suit, consisting of pants and a coat. Underneath, they layer as follows: long underwear, tops and bottoms; breeches, leather boots, and calf-length rubber boots; T-shirt, police shirt, leather jacket, scarf, and helmet. The Harley-Davidson mittens were great for keeping hands warm. Each finger had an individual slot within the mitten. In the winter, the motor officers experiment with just about everything to stay warm, including silk ski masks and anything else that might work. Motor officers remain outside for the full eight-hour shift. They dress so warmly that they really don't want to be inside.

The duties of Pittsburgh motor officers consist of escort, traffic enforcement, and traffic control. They escort all dignitaries and politicians, including the President and Vice President, from downtown Pittsburgh out to the greater Pittsburgh Airport and back again, depending on their needs. Other duties include accident investigation, crowd control, special events, football and baseball games, rock shows, and rush hour traffic. Pursuits are discouraged. Instead, they stay behind the vehicle in question and give the patrol cars the location. The speeder eventually finds himself boxed in by the patrol cars.

Without the sidecar, the FXRP can be easily maneuvered on the sidewalks, if necessary, when downtown traffic is heavy and motor officers are needed for an emergency at another location. The

addition of a sidecar has its special advantages. When controlling crowds along a parade route, a motor officer trying to get people out of the street and back up onto the sidewalk can use the sidecar as a sort of prod. Ofc. Rosemeyer once even used the sidecar to trip up a purse snatcher as the thief was running down the street.

In January 1993, Ofc. Rosemeyer was dressed for winter and riding with the sidecar. He was making a left-hand turn in the downtown area, when the sidecar broke away from the bike. The front of the sidecar broke and fell to the street, with the bike on top of the sidecar. Rider, motor, and sidecar just slid down the road until they crashed. Ofc. Rosemeyer suffered broken ribs, a crushed knee, and a neck injury. After

One of the tools of the trade for today's motor officer is radar, or in this case, laser. This unit is easy to use and difficult for the speeder to evade. The officer places the red dot on the vehicle and the numbers pop up. Unlike the old-style radar that projects a beam that a radar detector can pick up, the narrow laser beam can track a vehicle without setting off an alarm in the speeder's car.

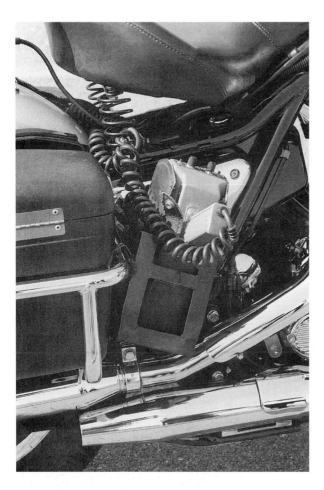

Radar/laser mount for the FXRP.

about two months, he was fine and back at work on the motorcycle. That was the first time the sidecar had ever broken free in all his years riding motors for the department.

Motor Officer Andrea Smyth

Officer Andrea Smyth joined the Las Vegas Metropolitan Police Department as a patrol officer in 1989. After three-and-a-half years patrolling in a car, she applied for the position of motor officer. Having raced Yamaha and Kawasaki dirt bikes off-road for more than ten years, the transition to the seat of a Harley was second nature. She is presently riding a 1988 Harley-Davidson FXRP with 42,000 miles on it. At 50,000, she will be issued another bike, and, as far as she's concerned, it had better be a Harley.

Ofc. Smyth explained that procedures for a routine traffic stop done from a motorcycle are different from those followed by patrol officers riding in a squad car. The issue of officer safety is paramount and governs everything. First, officers have virtually no protection on a motorcycle

compared to what they have with a car. In addition, the violator is slow in recognizing a single motorcycle in the rearview mirror, and other vehicles on the road do not easily see a motorcycle, even though the red lights and sirens are activated. The motor officer is taught to dismount only when the vehicle in question has come to a complete stop. Then, the officer informs dispatch of the location. Some departments teach officers to dismount on the high side of the motorcycle to minimize the risk of stepping into traffic. Officers have to watch the behavior of the driver and vehicle occupants at all times, because the motorcycle provides very little cover.

When approaching the vehicle, the motor officer must be aware of oncoming traffic at her back. Because the motorcycle parked behind the car is so small, drivers of other vehicles do not see it right away, and do not realize until it's too late that there is a human being standing next to the stopped car. Once alongside, the motor officer stands in front of the door hinge, behind the mirror. This way, she can see the driver, occupants of the vehicle, and all on-coming traffic. On a couple of occasions, Ofc. Smyth narrowly escaped being hit by an oncoming vehicle whose driver just didn't see her. Another disadvantage for a motor officer is the lack of a set of spotlights normally found on the A-pillars of police vehicles. This makes night stops even more risky.

In the case of a pursuit, motor officers are taught to handle it differently than if they were in a squad car. Although policies vary from department to department, generally speaking, high-speed pursuits by motor officers are discouraged. The goal is to follow close enough to get a license plate number, then drop back to a safe distance and give the location to dispatch, who can call a patrol car or the air unit to pick up the chase. Some officers will stay with the chase until the end, but the risk of injury is very high. The inherent danger is that other vehicles on the highway or roadway just don't see the motorcycle. It's up to each officer to ride within the limits of his or her expertise and the ability of the machine. They have to know when to stop.

Ofc. Smyth attests to the high level of respect motor officers receive from the drivers they stop. Everybody asks about the motorcycle, and when they find out it's a Harley, they want to get out and take a look. Some even ask for a ride and start "yakking" about the bike as their ticket is being written!

One summer, the deputy chief asked the traffic division for two motor officers to help patrol Las Vegas Boulevard on Friday and Saturday nights when the boulevard is at a virtual standstill due to gridlock. Ofc. Smyth and her partner volunteered. Because of the traffic congestion, the motor officers split traffic lanes and rode on the sidewalks and medians. Although some members of the bicycle patrol who normally patrol this area had received motorcycle training, they found the motorcycles too big, and expressed wonder at the motor officers who could maneuver so easily under such conditions. Ofc. Smyth loves the smooth ride of the FXRP, and although she rides forty hours each week, she is still up for more. "One of these days," she promises, "I will own a Harley-Davidson...most definitely."

Motorcycle Training for Police Motor Officers

Every single motor officer on patrol today should attend some sort of motorcycle training course before beginning on-the-job training with his or her department. In the early days, such training was unheard of. The leap from a bicycle to a motorcycle was not seen as anything extraordinary. The inherent dangers were accepted as part of the job, with little thought toward preventing accidents and injuries unique to motorcycle patrol.

Retired Motor Officer Rod Welsh recalled that as far back as 1936, when he first rode Harleys for the Long Beach Police Department, there was no formalized motorcycle training. Sgt. Welsh did not know how to ride a motorcycle when he received word that he was to report for motor duty in three weeks. He got one of the current motor officers to show him how to ride. He was told that it was just like riding a bicycle, except that you had to activate it. Official departmental training consisted of spending two weeks riding with a senior motor officer. After that, you were on your own.

We know that the Los Angeles Police Department had a two-week formalized motorcycle

The EVO, or Blockhead, motor powers today's police Harleys.

Two motor officers from the Richmond Police motor unit pose on their FXRPs in front of St. John's Church, a registered National Landmark erected in 1741. In this church, on March 23, 1775, Patrick Henry kindled the torch of liberty with his words, "Give me liberty...or give me death!" *Richmond, Virginia, Police Archives*

law enforcement work. Although the course was developed for the CHP, the expertise has always been available to other agencies.

Today, numerous training centers throughout the country specialize in motorcycle operation as it relates to law enforcement. The Northwestern University Traffic Institute, in conjunction with Harley-Davidson Motor Company, operates a National Motorcycle Academy, offering one- and two-week courses. The California Highway Patrol offers its course to members of all agencies, as does the San Bernardino County Sheriff's Department at their new, state-of-the-art training facility in Southern California.

The fact that someone may have prior experience riding a motorcycle as a civilian does not guarantee they possess the mental or physical skills necessary to operate a motorcycle for police work. Police motorcycles have a load factor much higher than that of a pleasure cruiser. The distribution of that load is also unusual, resulting in some unique handling problems. Safe operation at high speed and maneuverability at slow speeds use skills that remain undeveloped in most civilian riders. The technology of the motorcycle generally exceeds the abilities of most riders.

Some basic techniques are taught to potential motor officers to make them better riders with enough expertise to avoid or minimize potential accidents. We cite information from the San Bernardino County Sheriff's Department's Basic Motorcycle Training Course taught at their training facility.

Failure to learn specific techniques leads to the inevitable consequences. For example, failure to learn proper head and eye placement (i.e., looking where you want to go, instead of where you are) will result in improper positioning, lack of control, and hitting objects. Failure to coordinate clutch and throttle (i.e., finding the friction point) will result in lack of control, motor stalling, dumping the bike, damage, and injury. Failure to master controlled braking (i.e., proper use of both brakes) will result in not slowing fast enough, locking one or both brakes, brake fade, collision, crash, and injury. Failure to learn to keep both feet on the footboards, not on the ground, will result in lack of control, injury to

RIGHT
Six additional red flashing lights and a large strobe on the back of the radio box are installed on this FXRP. The license plate gives an insight into this officer's attitude.

training program at least as far back as 1947. The first week consisted of vehicle code training, with the second week devoted to riding the motorcycle. Bob Hale, a retired motor officer with the LAPD, first trained on a 1947 Knucklehead. In those days, you had to crank the engine. He remembers that in training, officers were taught to crank it as fast as you could, get it in gear, and get going, all in one smooth motion. He remembers spinning donuts around rubber cones and pylons, intentionally placed too close together to force riders to break traction on the dirt course. Then for high-speed training, they would zoom down the runways at the old Air National Guard facility. Obstacles were thrown into the path of the riders, who practiced taking evasive action.

The California Highway Patrol developed its first motor officer training program in 1968 to teach the safe, effective use of motorcycles for

The transmission of this 1993 FXRP has aftermarket trim added. Motor officers take a great deal of pride in their machines. It's not unusual for an officer to "customize" his motorcycle with a little extra chrome.

foot, poor clutch/throttle control, and lack of confidence.

Safety and the importance of defensive riding are stressed in all motorcycle training courses for motor officers. Understanding how and why most motorcycle accidents occur helps the motor officer grasp the importance of mastering the above mentioned skills. The Hurt Study is often cited for statistics on the primary causes of motorcycle accidents in the general motorcycle riding population. Obvious correlations can be made for police officers riding motors. The report is officially titled, "Motorcycle Accident Cause Factors and Identification of Countermeasures. Volume I: Technical Report" (Hurt, H. H., Ouellet, J. V., and Thom, D. R.; Traffic Safety Center, University of Southern California, Los Angeles, California, 90007; Contract No. DOT HS-5-01160, January 1981, Final Report).

To compile results, the team of researchers investigated 900 motorcycle accidents in the Los Angeles area and analyzed an additional 3,600 motorcycle traffic accident reports in the same geographic area. We quote from this report as follows:

• Approximately three-fourths of these motorcycle accidents involved collision with another vehicle, which was most usually a passenger automobile.
• In the single vehicle accidents, motorcycle rider error was present as the accident precipitating factor in about two-thirds of the cases, with the typical error being a slide-out and fall due to overbraking or running wide on a curve due to excess speed or under-cornering.
• In the multiple vehicle accidents, the driver of the other vehicle violated the motorcycle right-of-way and caused the accident in two-thirds of those accidents.
• The failure of motorists to detect and recognize motorcycles in traffic is the predominating cause of motorcycle accidents. The driver of the other vehicle involved in the collision with the motorcycle did not see the motorcycle before the collision, or did not see the motorcycle until too late to avoid the collision.
• The most frequent accident configuration is the motorcycle proceeding straight, then

the automobile makes a left turn in front of the oncoming motorcycle.
• Intersections are the most likely place for the motorcycle accident, with the other vehicle violating the motorcycle right-of-way, often violating traffic controls.
• The median pre-crash speed was 29.8mph, and the median crash speed was 21.5mph, and the one-in-a-thousand crash speed is approximately 86mph.
• The motorcycle riders involved in accidents are essentially without training; 92 percent were self-taught or learned from family or friends.
• Motorcycle riders in these accidents showed significant collision avoidance problems. Most riders overbraked and skidded the rear wheel and underbraked the front wheel, greatly reducing collision avoidance deceleration. The ability to countersteer and swerve was essentially absent.
• The typical motorcycle accident allows the motorcyclist just less than two seconds to complete all collision avoidance action.
• The large displacement motorcycles are underrepresented in accidents, but they are associated with higher injury severity when involved in accidents.

What follows is a description of various drills used at the San Bernardino County Sheriff's Department's training facility in the basic course for police officers assigned to ride motors—keep your feet up and don't touch the cones!

The Figure Eight drill teaches balance and coordination and simulates in-field turning maneuvers in small areas. The instructor watches for smooth application of throttle and clutch and balance. The student's feet should not touch the ground.

The Eighteen-Foot Enclosed Circle drill teaches control of the motorcycle at extreme slow speed in a confined area, with lock to lock turn a requirement. The instructor watches for smooth, slow operation of the motorcycle and proper application of the throttle, clutch, and rear brake. The student's feet should not touch the ground.

The Off-Set Ninety-Degree Turns (flat surface/incline) drill teaches proper balance, control, and coordination of clutch, throttle, and rear brake. This drill inspires confidence on the part of the student in control of the motorcycle while making turning movements on a flat or in-

With his right hand rolling on the V-twin power, Ofc. Wisehart of the Hemet (California) Police Department enters the high-speed track of the San Bernardino County Sheriff's Department's training facility. On this particular day, Ofc. Wisehart was serving as a motorcycle training instructor.

clined street. The instructor looks for the proper application of clutch, throttle, and rear brake (used only on the downside of the incline turn). In addition, feet should be on footboards and head and eye placement should be as demonstrated.

The Intersection drill teaches control at slow speeds and assists in beginning lock to lock turns. The instructor looks for proper balance and proper clutch and throttle application. The student should be able to use the throttle to keep the motorcycle upright. Feet should not touch the ground.

The Long (and Short) Cone Weave drill teaches balance, control, and coordination of clutch, throttle, and brake. This drill represents a heavy traffic situation where the rider must look ahead while frequently changing lanes. The instructor looks for smoothness and control during lock to lock turns. A rhythm should develop. No elongated, sweeping turns should be used. The distance between cones is 10 feet 4 inches for the long cone weave, and 9 feet 6 inches for the short cone weave.

Stopping and Turning (flat surface/incline). This exercise teaches balance, control, and coordination of throttle and clutch while turning from a stopped position. The student comes to a stop and, without stalling or putting a foot down, accelerates into an immediate right or left turn. The instructor looks for a smooth stop and proper balance when stopped, smooth clutch/throttle control, proper balance while turning, no stalling, no dragging of feet, proper head and eye placement, and no braking. To increase the degree of difficulty, the same exercise is repeated on an incline, where braking is acceptable in order to hold the incline.

The "S" Curve drill (four drills, progressing from easy to most difficult) uses a coned, weave pattern with lock to lock turns to change direction. This drill simulates in-town traffic conditions at slow speeds, where the officer must weave between vehicles. The instructor looks for a smooth, flowing motion through the patterns. Students tend to stall the engine or drop the motorcycle due to the slow speeds.

touch the ground and no brakes. The rider should slalom in a smooth, flowing motion.

The "U" Turns/Pairs "U" Turns exercises teach control of motorcycles riding in pairs within a limited space while turning. The student enters a left-turn pocket, completes a "U" turn, then proceeds to another left turn pocket. The motorcycle is to remain upright, then leaned in the direction of the "U" turn.

The Slow Ride drill teaches balance at extremely slow speed in heavy traffic situations. The student must ride in a straight line as slow as possible. The instructor watches for lateral movement to keep speed down. The student should not over-rev the engine, but maintain proper coordination of clutch and throttle. Feet should not touch the ground. A slow ride/no brake exercise has the student entering a 50-foot-by-4-foot

Our "dirt-cam" view of motorcycle training. In the early days, all one needed to know was how to balance on two wheels. Today's training consists of a grueling series of intense, low-speed drills, along with some science and a lot of common sense.

The instructor coaches smooth coordination of clutch and throttle. Feet should not touch the ground.

The 30mph Cone Weave teaches balance and collision avoidance. At a speed of about 30mph, the student weaves through the straight line pattern using the countersteering technique. This exercise represents a heavy traffic situation, lane changing, and looking ahead. The instructor watches for a slight pressure of the hand on the inside of the handlebar in the direction of travel (push right, go right). Feet should not

Training officers watch their student riders closely and provide immediate verbal feedback throughout each drill. This officer takes his FXRP through the "S" curve drill, simulating in-town traffic conditions at low speeds. Instructors, all current or former motor officers, monitor the skill level of each rider as he or she attempts each drill.

Officer Tony Spates of the Hemet (California) Police Department maneuvers his FXRP through a cone pattern. Showing good form, he sits straight, knees tight to the tank, with head and eyes looking in the direction of the next cone in the pattern. The safety guards have been taped to protect the chrome from an occasional spill. Virtually everyone will drop a bike during this two-week course.

area, and remaining inside as long as possible, without braking.

The Dirt Riding exercise sharpens control and coordination on less than ideal surfaces. Students follow an instructor along an off-road course incorporating gravel, sand, dirt, deep ruts, trenches, washboard surfaces, and steep inclines. Instructors look for student judgment and the tendency to override present capabilities.

The Board Drag drill allows the student to gain confidence in leaning the motorcycle to maximum angle and represents limited turning situations in field operations. The instructor looks for proper balance and throttle/clutch application, and use of the throttle to keep the motorcycle upright.

The Broad Slides exercise simulates handling characteristics during a locked rear skid. Students proceed in a straight upright position through a series of cones, locking up the rear brake only. The maximum speed for this exercise is 15mph. Students learn proper control of the motorcycle in panic stop ("Oh, s—t") situations encountered on the street.

Stopping on a Curve inspires confidence of the rider in controlling the stopping or braking ability of the motorcycle in a leaning mode. The instructor looks for smooth operation of the mo-

THE HARLEY-DAVIDSON® FXRP PURSUIT GLIDE™

THE HARLEY-DAVIDSON® FXRP PURSUIT GLIDE™ (WINDSHIELD MODEL).

A TURN OF THE WRIST AND THE FXRP PURSUIT GLIDE™ JUMPS TO LIFE, PROVIDING IMMEDIATE REACTION ANY TIME DUTY CALLS. ITS RELIABLE V2® EVOLUTION® ENGINE AND DURABLE CHASSIS ARE PERFECTLY SUITED TO THE RIGORS OF POLICE WORK. AND WITH ITS CLASSIC LOOK AND DISTINCTIVE SOUND, IT CARRIES THE JOB OFF IN HIGH STYLE.

FRAME-MOUNTED FAIRING OPTION FEATURED ON THE FXRP PURSUIT GLIDE™.

PERFORMANCE

- AIR COOLED, 4 STROKE V2® EVOLUTION® ENGINE, 80 CUBIC INCHES OF POLICE PERFORMANCE AND POWER
- KEVLAR® REINFORCED BELT FINAL DRIVE MAINTAINS MAXIMUM EFFICIENCY AND BELT LIFE WITH MINIMAL ADJUSTMENT

- AGILE, EASILY MANEUVERABLE IN ALL TRAFFIC SITUATIONS
- HIGH PERFORMANCE CLUTCH PERFORMS EQUALLY WELL IN URBAN PATROL AND HIGHWAY DUTY

COMFORT

- SOLO-SUSPENDED SEAT FOR ALL DAY COMFORT
- INDIVIDUALLY ADJUSTABLE CLUTCH AND BRAKE LEVERS
- WIND TUNNEL TESTED, FRAME MOUNTED FAIRING AVAILABLE FOR REDUCED RIDER FATIGUE
- FLOORBOARDS FOR ADDED COMFORT

DEPENDABILITY

- DUAL-DISC FRONT BRAKES PROVIDE EXCELLENT STOPPING POWER
- AVAILABILITY OF SPECIAL EXTRA LOUD AIR HORN HOOK-UP TO SIREN/PUBLIC ADDRESS SYSTEM*
- VARIETY OF HIGH VISIBILITY STROBE PACKAGES AVAILABLE*

- CLUTCH INTERLOCK TO PREVENT STARTING IN GEAR

VALUE

- BUILT AND DESIGNED TO PROVIDE YEARS OF RELIABLE SERVICE
- LOW MAINTENANCE COSTS
- HIGH RESALE VALUE
- 55 MPG HIGHWAY AND 43 MPG CITY**

*AVAILABLE THROUGH YOUR DEALER

**BASED ON OUR OWN TESTS. ACTUAL MILEAGE MAY VARY DEPENDING ON RIDING HABITS, WEATHER CONDITIONS AND TRIP LENGTH.

WE CARE ABOUT YOU. BE SURE TO RIDE SAFELY AND WITHIN THE LIMITS OF YOUR ABILITIES. RIDE WITH YOUR HEADLIGHT ON AND WATCH OUT FOR THE OTHER PERSON. ALWAYS WEAR A HELMET, PROPER EYEWEAR AND APPROPRIATE CLOTHING. NEVER RIDE WHILE UNDER THE INFLUENCE OF ALCOHOL OR DRUGS. KNOW YOUR OWN HARLEY® AND READ AND UNDERSTAND YOUR OWNER'S MANUAL FROM COVER TO COVER. TO CONTACT THE HARLEY-DAVIDSON® DEALER IN YOUR AREA CALL TOLL FREE 1-800-443-2153 IN THE U.S.A. ALL RIGHTS RESERVED.
PRINTED IN THE U.S.A. ©1992 HARLEY-DAVIDSON, INC.

HARLEY-DAVIDSON® POLICE MOTORCYCLES

THE HARLEY-DAVIDSON® FLHTP ELECTRA GLIDE®

The Harley-Davidson® FLHTP Electra Glide® (windshield model).

The ultimate police motorcycle. The legendary FLHTP Electra Glide®. It's the latest evolution in our top-of-the-line police motorcycle, with the distinctive form and time-proven function you expect. Powered by 80 cubic inches of Milwaukee's finest, it creates a presence unequaled by any other machine.

Fork-mounted fairing option featured on the FLHTP Electra Glide®.

PERFORMANCE	COMFORT	DEPENDABILITY	VALUE
▪ Air-cooled, four stroke V2® Evolution® engine suited to the rigors of police work	▪ Engine-isolating tri-mount chassis to intercept engine vibration and reduce rider fatigue	▪ Massive 11.5 inch dual front disc brake rotors provide excellent stopping power	▪ Built and designed to provide years of reliable service
▪ Kevlar® reinforced belt final drive maintains maximum efficiency and belt life with minimal adjustment	▪ Solo-suspended air saddle for long hours on the road	▪ Availability of special extra loud air horn hook-up to siren/public address system*	▪ Low maintenance costs
▪ Heavy-duty, air-adjustable anti-dive front suspension and air-adjustable rear suspension	▪ Individually adjustable clutch and brake levers	▪ Variety of high visibility strobe packages available*	▪ High resale value
▪ Spacious saddlebags are lockable and hinged. Special designed quick-fastener makes for easy opening and closing	▪ Three-point adjustable floorboards for maximum rider comfort	▪ Clutch interlock to prevent starting in gear	▪ 50 MPG highway and 39 MPG city**
		▪ Waterproof electrical connectors	
		▪ Automatic fuel shut off valve	

HARLEY-DAVIDSON® ⬥ POLICE MOTORCYCLES

*Available through your dealer **Based on our own tests. Actual mileage may vary depending on riding habits, weather conditions and trip length. We care about you. Be sure to ride safely and within the limits of your abilities. Ride with your headlight on and watch out for the other person. Always wear a helmet, proper eyewear and appropriate clothing. Never ride while under the influence of alcohol or drugs. Know your own Harley® and read and understand your owner's manual from cover to cover. To contact the Harley-Davidson® dealer in your area call toll free 1-800-443-2153 in the U.S.A. All rights reserved. ©1994 Harley-Davidson, Inc.

PREVIOUS PAGES LEFT
1994 was the last year for the FXRP Pursuit
Glide. *Harley-Davidson Motor Company*

PREVIOUS PAGES RIGHT
The tradition continues with the 1995
Electra-Glide police motorcycle. *Harley-Davidson Motor Company*

torcycle, proper application of both front and rear brakes (all fingers on front brake), and proper application of throttle and clutch. Students should watch speed and downshift.

Countersteering teaches students to use methods other than braking to avoid accidents. Students must be able to lean the motorcycle in a given direction by applying pressure to the appropriate handgrip. This exercise also teaches students to keep head and eyes up. The instructor demonstrates by riding toward the students. The instructor pushes the left handlebar to the left just prior to reaching the students. They observe that the front wheel will first go right, but then the motorcycle turns left. Students are reminded to give sufficient pressure on the inside of the handlebar grip to deflect the front wheel. Students should not counteract weight shift by opposite body lean and should not brake or lean sharply in both parts of the exercise. Speed is constant with feet firmly on footboards.

The Apexing drill teaches students to increase speed and lean in a curve in order to decrease the radius of a curve, and that if brakes are used while in a curve, the motorcycle will go wide and want to straighten up. The student must be able to maintain an entrance speed to a curve, apexing down to the center line, then increase the speed at the exit of the curve to straighten up the motorcycle. The student must be able to cause the motorcycle to lean to a given direction by applying pressure to the appropriate handgrip. This drill also teaches students to look up and through curves.

Motor officers who have taken these specialized training courses come away having learned things that could one day save their lives or at least minimize injury. Even officers who have ridden motorcycles for years benefit from new training techniques. Officers were once taught to lay the bike down in anticipation of a crash. Today, they are taught to use both the front and rear brakes and to avoid sliding either tire. Understanding the scientific physical characteristics of bodies in motion leads to the application of techniques that result in safer riding.

During the training course offered by Harley-Davidson Motor Company in conjunction with the Northwestern University Traffic Institute, a team of mechanics is on site each day to monitor the condition of the motorcycles and to repair them as necessary. The training exercises themselves serve as ongoing laboratory work for designers and mechanics. Harley-Davidson provides new motorcycles for the classes and then tears them down afterward to analyze stress points. Clutches and brakes take a beating during this course. The student motor officers run an average of 1500 to 2000rpm most of the time.

In all courses designed for law enforcement motor officers, there is an intense level of competition among students to excel. Often a matter of personal pride, students will spend extra time "after school" drilling with fellow officers. Body aches and pains in the areas of the neck, shoulders, arms, and hands are not unusual, as is the overall frustration level if things do not go just perfect.

The grading and evaluation standards are set to ensure that those who pass are fully qualified and safe in all areas. Those who do not pass are either not motorcycle material or have not quite mastered the necessary skills to ride safely. There is no favoritism extended to nice guys. You are either qualified and safe, or you shouldn't be riding a motorcycle.

EPILOGUE

Today, the Harley-Davidson police motorcycle is designed with the help of motor officers who ride daily in the field. With the creation of the Police Advisory Council in 1992, Harley-Davidson Motor Company conducts an ongoing effort to respond to its law enforcement customers. In conjunction with Northwestern University Traffic Institute, Harley-Davidson stays in touch with the needs of motor officers through ongoing motorcycle operator training courses. During these courses, mechanics and engineers can witness firsthand the impact of police duty on clutches and brake systems. The ongoing publication of *The Mounted Officer* is another way for Harley-Davidson to keep in touch with its police customers.

Presently, sales to police agencies represent about three percent of total sales. Harley-Davidson counts over 900 law enforcement agencies among its customers throughout North America. Harley-Davidson police motorcycles are purchased by departments in over twenty foreign countries. The Mexico City Police Department ranks as one of their biggest customers, with three divisions of police using the product. The Korean National Police is also among the largest users, with approximately 1,500 units in service.

In the United States, New York City is Harley's biggest law enforcement customer. Following New York, the state of Florida has become a hotbed of motorcycle activity, with over ninety police agencies being served. Florida is followed by Texas and California as the next big users of Harley-Davidson police motorcycles. Harley-Davidson estimates that about thirty-five percent of the police motorcycles sold in California (once its biggest U.S. customer) are Harleys. Sales are strong, however, in Northern California. Smaller departments surrounding Los Angeles and throughout the state, for that matter, also ride Harleys. Flexible buy-back agreements can make ownership of Harleys cost effective to many departments because of their favorable resale value.

Over time, the Harley-Davidson police motorcycle has changed much more than has the motor officer who rides it on patrol. With each new development or innovation, we have watched the machine become safer and more comfortable, powerful, and reliable. The early motor officers who rode without benefit of suspension, electric starters, or radios are to be admired. Their job was inherently dangerous. With each improvement, the motor officer's job became easier as the machine became a better tool.

The profile of the motor officer, however, has changed little. Motor officers are still confident, capable, and independent individuals who like their freedom yet enjoy being part of an elite team. They need a level of activity and stimulation that does not exist in an office setting. Unlike the daredevils of the early years, today's motor officer is a highly trained professional. They have earned our affection and admiration.

BOOKS:

Bolfert, Thomas C., *The Big Book of Harley-Davidson.* Harley-Davidson, Inc., 1991.

Bach, Sharon and Osterman, Ken, *The Legend Begins.* Harley-Davidson, Inc., 1993.

Hatfield, Jerry *Inside Harley-Davidson.* Motorbooks International, 1990.

Wright, David K., *The Harley-Davidson Motor Company: An Official Eighty-Year History.* Motorbooks International, 1987.

McCord, Monty, *Police Cars: A Photographic History.* Krause Publications, 1991.

Weisner, Wolfgang, *Harley-Davidson Photographic History.* Motorbooks International, 1989.

Wick, Robert A., *The California Highway Patrol: Yesterday and Today.* Phase Three Publishing, 1989.

Heyden Patricia E., *Behind the Badge: The History of the Lansing Police Department...* Lansing: Stuart Publishing, 1991.

Rosenblum, Martin Jack, *The Holy Ranger: Harley-Davidson Poems.* Ranger International Productions/Lion Publishing/Roar Recording, 1989.

Brinkerhoff, Stephen, *Motorcycle Training: Basic Course.* San Bernardino County Sheriff's Emergency Vehicle Operations Training Center. Revised July 1, 1994.

MAGAZINES:

Karger, George, "Dallas Motorcycle Brigade." *Motorcyclist,* February, 1957.

Phillips, Stephen, "That Vroom You Hear is Honda Motorcycles." *Business Week,* September 3, 1990.

"How Harley Beat Back the Japanese." *Fortune,* September 25, 1989. Books excerpt from *Well Made in America,* by Peter C. Reid.

Falconer, Erik, "Harley Spotter's Guide: How to Tell One Hog from Another." *Hot Rod Magazine,* December, 1993.

Watson, Peter, "Highway Patrol." *The Classic Motorcycle,* December, 1993.

"Harley-Davidson Spends $80 million on Quality." *Quality Progress,* January 1992.

Falconer, Erik. "How to Buy a Used Bike." *Hot Rod Magazine,* January 1994.

Lovell, Buck, "The American Cop Bike." *Hot Bike,* March 1992.

"90 Years of Harley-Davidson," *American Iron Magazine.* July 1993.

"90-Year Harley History," *American Rider,* Winter 1994.

The Mounted Officer Fall/Winter, 1992.

The Mounted Officer, Spring/Summer, 1993.

The Mounted Officer, Fall/Winter, 1993.

The Enthusiast, December 1943.

The Enthusiast, May 1948.

The Enthusiast, November 1948.

NEWSPAPERS:

Cummings, Judith, "California Patrol is Saddling Up on Harleys Again." *The New York Times,* January 8,1984.

Parachini, Allan, "Revving Up Motorcycle Wars: Harley Challenging Kawasaki Police Dominance." *Los Angeles Times,* September 4,1983.

Uris, Robin, "It's the Biggest Rush: Motorcycle Patrol draws Interest." *Courier-Post,* July 17,1992.

Squyres, Ann, "VIPs Get Harley-Davidson Treatment." *Southtown Economist,* November 23,1992.